Some adventures of Captain Simon Suggs : late of the Tallapoosa volunteers : together with "Taking the census," and other Alabama sketches.

Johnson Jones Hooper

SIMON SUGGS

ADVENTURES OF

CAPTAIN SIMON SUGGS,

TAKING THE CENSUS, ETC.

"... stand the dish ... e "them's th ... verest dogs in this country"
Page 131

PHILADELPHIA

SOME ADVENTURES

OF

CAPTAIN SIMON SUGGS,

LATE OF

THE TALLAPOOSA VOLUNTEERS;

TOGETHER WITH

"TAKING THE CENSUS,"

AND

OTHER ALABAMA SKETCHES.

BY A COUNTRY EDITOR.

WITH A PORTRAIT FROM LIFE, AND OTHER ILLUSTRATIONS,
BY DARLEY.

"— Si tantus amor scribendi te rapit, aude,
Cæsaris invicti res dicere "—Hor.

If you *must* scribble something—let it be, sir,
The mighty deeds of the unconquer'd Cæsar!

PHILADELPHIA:

CAREY AND HART.

1845.

PREFACE.

A small portion of " Captain Suggs," and one or two of the other sketches in this little volume, have already appeared in a country newspaper edited by the writer, and in the New York "Spirit of the Times." These having been somewhat flatteringly received by the public, the writer was induced to accede to a proposition to print in this form. " Suggs" has therefore been extended greatly beyond the original intention, and several new sketches added; so that by far the larger portion of the volume is published for the first time.

If what was at first designed, chiefly, to amuse a community unpretending in its tastes, shall amuse the Great Public, the writer will, of course, be gratified. If otherwise, his mortification will be lessened by the reflection that the fault of the obtrusion is not entirely his own.

La Fayette, Chambers County, Ala.
March, 1845.

TO

WILLIAM T. PORTER, Esq.,

EDITOR OF THE NEW YORK SPIRIT OF THE TIMES,

THE FOLLOWING PAGES

ARE

RESPECTFULLY INSCRIBED,

AS WELL IN TOKEN

OF THE WRITER'S REGARD,

AS BECAUSE,

IF THERE BE HUMOUR IN THEM, •

THEY COULD HAVE NO MORE

APPROPRIATE DEDICATION

CAPTAIN SIMON SUGGS.

~~~~~~~~~~~~

CHAPTER FIRST.

INTRODUCTION—SIMON PLAYS THE "SNATCH" GAME.

It is not often that the living worthy furnishes a theme for the biographer's pen. The pious task of commemorating the acts, and depicting the character of the great or good, is generally and properly deferred until they are past blushing, or swearing—constrained to a decorous behaviour by the folds of their cerements. Were it otherwise, who could estimate the pangs of wounded modesty which would result! Who could say how keen would be the mortification, or how crimson the cheek of Grocer Tibbetts, for instance, should we present him to the world in all the resplendent glory of his public and his private virtues!—dragging him, as it were, from the bosom of retirement and Mrs. Tibbetts, to hold him up before the full gaze of "the community," with all his qualities, characteristics, and peculiarities written on a large label and pasted to his forehead! Would'nt Mr. Tibbetts almost die of bashfulness? And would'nt Mrs. Tibbetts tell all her neighbours, that she would just as soon they had put Mr. Tibbetts in the stocks, if it were not for the concomitant little boys and rotten eggs? Certainly: and Mrs. Tabitha Tibbetts in making such a remark, would be impelled by a principle which exists in a majority of human minds—a principle which makes the idea revolting, that every body should know all about us in our life-times, notwithstanding our characters may present something better even than a fair average of virtue and talent.

But "there is no rule without an exception," and notwithstanding that it is both unusual and improper, generally, to publish biographies of remarkable personages during their lives, for the reason already explained, as well as because such histories must, of necessity, be incomplete and require *post mortem* additions—notwithstanding all this, we say, there are cases and persons, in which and to whom, the general rule cannot be considered to apply. Take, by way of illustration, the case of a candidate for office —for the Presidency we'll say. His life, up to the time when his reluctant acquiescence in the wishes of his friends was wrung from him, by the stern demands of a self-immolating patriotism, MUST be written. It is an absolute, political necessity. His enemies *will* know enough to attack; his friends *must* know enough to defend.—Thus Jackson, Van Buren, Clay, and Polk have each a biography published while they live. Nay, the thing has been carried further; and in the first of each "Life" there is found what is termed a "counterfeit presentment" of the subject of the pages which follow. And so, not only are the moral and intellectual endowments of the candidate heralded to the world of voters; but an attempt is made to create an idea of his *physique*. By this means, all the country has in its mind's eye, an image of a little gentleman with a round, oily face—sleek, bald pate, delicate whiskers, and foxy smile, which they call Martin Van Buren; and future generations of naughty children who will persist in sitting up when they should be a-bed, will be frightened to their cribs by the lithograph of "Major General Andrew Jackson," which their mammas will declare to be a faithful representation of the Evil One—an atrocious slander, by the bye, on the potent, and comparatively well-favoured, prince of the infernal world.

What we have said in the preceding paragraphs was intended to prepare the minds of our readers for the reception of the fact, that we have not undertaken to furnish for their amusement and instruction, in this and the chapters which shall come after, a few incidents—for we are by far too modest to attempt a connected memoir—in the life of Captain Simon Suggs, of Tallapoosa, without the profoundest meditation on the propriety of doing so ere the captain has been "gathered to his fathers." No! no! we have chewed the cud of this matter, until we flatter ourself all its juices have been expressed; and the result is, that as Captain Simon Suggs thinks it "more than probable" he shall "come before the people of Tallapoosa" in the course of a year or two, he is, in our opinion, clearly "within the line of safe precedents," and bound in *honor* to furnish the Suggs party with such information respecting himself, as will enable them to vindicate his character whenever and wherever it may be attacked by the ruthless and pol-

luted tongues of Captain Simon Suggs' enemies. And
in order that our hero should not appear before his
fellow citizens under circumstances less advantageous
than those which mark the introduction to the public
of other distinguished individuals, we have, at the
outlay of much trouble and expense, obtained the services of an artist competent to delineate his countenance, so that all who have never yet seen the Captain may be able to recognize him immediately
whenever it shall be their good fortune to be inducted
into his presence.   His autograph,—which was only
produced unblotted and in orthographical correctness,
after three several efforts, "from a rest," on the
counter of Bill Griffin's confectionary—we have presented with a view to humor the whim of those who
fancy they can read character in a signature.   All
such, we suspect, would pronounce the Captain *rug-
ged, stubborn, and austere* in his disposition ; whereas
in fact, he is *smooth, even-tempered, and facile!*

In aid of the portrait, however, it is necessary we
should add a verbal description, in order to perfect
the reader's conceptions of the Captain.

Beginning then, at our friend Simon's intellectual
extremity :—His head is somewhat large, and thinly
covered with coarse, silver-white hair, a single lock
of which lies close and smooth down the middle of a
forehead which is thus divided into a couple of very
acute triangles, the base of each of which is an eye-
brow, lightly defined, and seeming to owe its scantiness to the depilatory assistance of a pair of tweezers.
Beneath these almost shrubless cliffs, a pair of eyes
with light-grey pupils and variegated whites, dance

and twinkle in an aqueous humor which is constantly distilling from the corners. Lids without lashes complete the optical apparatus of Captain Suggs ; and the edges of these, always of a sanguineous hue, glow with a reduplicated brilliancy whenever the Captain has remained a week or so in town, or elsewhere in the immediate vicinity of any of those citizens whom the county court has vested with the important privilege of vending " spirituous liquors in less quantities than one quart." The nose we find in the neighbourhood of these eyes, is long and low, with an extremity of singular acuteness, overhanging the subjacent mouth. Across the middle, which is slightly raised, the skin is drawn with exceeding tightness, as if to contrast with the loose and wrinkled abundance supplied to the throat and chin. But the mouth of Captain Simon Suggs is his great feature, and measures about four inches horizontally. An ever-present sneer—not all malice, however—draws down the corners, from which radiate many small wrinkles that always testify to the Captain's love of the " filthy weed." A sharp chin monopolizes our friend's bristly, iron-gray beard. All these facial beauties are supported by a long and skinny, but muscular neck, which is inserted after the ordinary fashion in the upper part of a frame, lithe, long, and sinewy, and clad in Kentucky jeanes, a trifle worn. Add to all this, that our friend is about fifty years old, and seems to indurate as he advances in years, and our readers will have as accurate an idea of the personal appearance of Captain Simon Suggs, late of the Tallapoosa Volunteers, as we are able to give them.

The moral and intellectual qualities which, with the physical proportions we have endeavoured to portray, make up the entire entity of Captain Suggs, may be readily described. His whole ethical system lies snugly in his favourite aphorism—"IT IS GOOD TO BE SHIFTY IN A NEW COUNTRY"—which means that it is right and proper that one should live as merrily and as comfortably as possible at the expense of others; and of the practicability of this in particular instances, the Captain's whole life has been a long series of the most convincing illustrations. But notwithstanding this fundamental principle of Captain Suggs' philosophy, it were uncandid not to say that his actions often indicate the most benevolent emotions; and there are well-authenticated instances within our knowledge, wherein he has divided with a needy friend, the five or ten dollar bill which his consummate address had enabled him to obtain from some luckless individual, without the rendition of any sort of equivalent, excepting only solemnly reiterated promises to repay within two hours at farthest. To this amiable trait, and his riotous good-fellowship, the Captain is indebted for his great popularity among a certain class of his fellow citizens—that is, the class composed of the individuals with whom he divides the bank bills, and holds his wild nocturnal revelries.

The shifty Captain Suggs is a miracle of shrewdness. He possesses, in an eminent degree, that tact which enables man to detect the *soft spots* in his fellow, and to assimilate himself to whatever company he may fall in with. Besides, he has a quick, ready wit, which has extricated him from many an unpleasant predicament, and which makes him whenever he chooses to be so—and that is always—very companionable. In short, nature gave the Captain the precise intellectual outfit most to be desired by a man of his propensities. She sent him into the world a sort of he-Pallas, ready to cope with his kind, from his infancy, in all the arts by which men "*get along*" in the world; if she made him, in respect to his moral conformation, a beast of prey, she did not refine the cruelty by denying him the fangs and the claws.

But it is high time we were beginning to record some of those specimens of the worthy Captain's ingenuity, which entitle him to the epithet "*Shifty*." We shall therefore relate the earliest characteristic anecdote which we have been able to obtain; and we present it to our readers with assurances that it has come to our knowledge in such a way as to leave upon our mind not "a shadow of doubt" of its perfect genuineness. It will serve, if no other purpose, at least to illustrate the precocious development of Captain Suggs' peculiar talent.

Until Simon entered his seventeenth year, he lived with his father, an old "hard shell" Baptist preacher; who, though very pious and remarkably austere, was very avaricious. The old man reared his boys—or endeavoured to do so—according to the strictest requisitions of the moral law. But he lived, at the time to which we refer, in Middle Georgia, which was then newly settled; and Simon, whose wits from the time he was a "shirt-tail boy," were always too sharp for his father's, contrived to contract all the coarse vices incident to such a region. He stole his

mother's roosters to fight them at Bob Smith's grocery, and his father's plough-horses to enter them in
"quarter" matches at the same place. He pitched
dollars with Bob Smith himself, and could "beat him
into doll rags" whenever it came to a measurement.
To crown his accomplishments, Simon was tip-top at
the game of "old sledge," which was the fashionable
game of that era; and was early initiated in the mys-
teries of "stocking the papers." The vicious habits
of Simon were, of course, a sore trouble to his father,
Elder Jedediah. He reasoned, he counselled, he re-
monstrated, and he lashed—but Simon was an incor-
rigible, irreclaimable devil. One day the simple-
minded old man returned rather unexpectedly to the
field where he had left Simon and Ben and a negro
boy named Bill, at work. Ben was still following
his plough, but Simon and Bill were in a fence corner
very earnestly engaged at "seven up." Of course
the game was instantly suspended, as soon as they
spied the old man sixty or seventy yards off, striding
towards them.

It was evidently a "gone case" with Simon and
Bill; but our hero determined to make the best of it.
Putting the cards into one pocket, he coolly picked
up the small coins which constituted the stake, and
fobbed them in the other, remarking, "Well, Bill,
this game's blocked; we'd as well quit."

"But, mass Simon," remarked the boy, "half dat
money's mine. An't you gwine to lemme hab
'em?"

"Oh, never mind the money, Bill; the old man's
going to take the bark off both of us—and besides,

with the hand I helt when we quit. I should 'a beat you and won it all any way."

" Well, but mass Simon, we nebber finish de game, and de rule ———"

"Go to an orful h—l with your rule," said the impatient Simon—"don't you see daddy's right down upon us, with an armful of hickories? I tell you I helt nothin' but trumps, and could 'a beat the horns off of a billygoat. Don't that satisfy you? Somehow or another you're d—d hard to please!" About this time a thought struck Simon, and in a low tone —for by this time the Reverend Jedediah was close at hand—he continued, "But maybe daddy don't know, *right down sure*, what we've been doin'. Let's try him with a lie—twon't hurt, no way—let's tell him we've been playin' mumble-peg."

Bill was perforce compelled to submit to this inequitable adjustment of his claim to a share of the stakes; and of course agreed to swear to the game of mumble-peg. All this was settled and a peg driven into the ground, slyly and hurriedly, between Simon's legs as he sat on the ground, just as the old man reached the spot. He carried under his left arm, several neatly-trimmed sprouts of formidable length, while in his left hand he held one which he was intently engaged in divesting of its superfluous twigs.

" Soho! youngsters!—*you* in the fence corner, and the *crap* in the grass ; what saith the Scriptur', Simon? 'Go to the ant, thou sluggard,' and so forth and so on What in the round creation of the yeath have you and that nigger been a-doin'?"

Bill shook with fear, but Simon was cool as a cu-

cumber, and answered his father to the effect that they had been wasting a little time in the game of mumble-peg.

"Mumble-peg! mumble-peg!" repeated old Mr. Suggs, "what's that?"

Simon explained the process of *rooting* for the peg; how the operator got upon his knees, keeping his arms stiff by his sides, leaned forward and extracted the peg with his teeth.

"So you git *upon your knees*, do you, to pull up that nasty little stick! you'd better git upon 'em to ask mercy for your sinful souls and for a dyin' world. But let's see one o' you git the peg up now."

The first impulse of our hero was to volunteer to gratify the curiosity of his worthy sire, but a glance at the old man's countenance changed his "notion," and he remarked that "Bill was a long ways the best hand." Bill who did not deem Simon's modesty an omen very favourable to himself, was inclined to reciprocate compliments with his young master; but a gesture of impatience from the old man set him instantly upon his knees; and, bending forward, he essayed to lay hold with his teeth of the peg, which Simon, just at that moment, very wickedly pushed a half inch further down. Just as the breeches and hide of the boy were stretched to the uttermost, old Mr. Suggs brought down his longest hickory, with both hands, upon the precise spot where the tension was greatest. With a loud yell, Bill plunged forward, upsetting Simon, and rolled in the grass; rubbing the castigated part with fearful energy. Simon, though overthrown, was unhurt; and he was mentally complimenting himself upon the sagacity which had prevented his illustrating the game of mumble-peg for the paternal amusement, when his attention was arrested by the old man's stooping to pick up something—what is it?—a card upon which Simon had been sitting, and which, therefore, had not gone with the rest of the pack into his pocket. The simple Mr. Suggs had only a vague idea of the paste-board abomination called *cards;* and though he decidedly inclined to the opinion that this was one, he was by no means certain of the fact. Had Simon known this he would certainly have escaped; but he did not. His father assuming the look of extreme sapiency which is always worn by the interrogator who does not desire or expect to increase his knowledge by his questions, asked—

" What's this, Simon ?"

" The Jack-a-dimunts," promptly responded Simon, who gave up all as lost after this *faux pas.*

" What was it doin' down thar Simon, my sonny?" continued Mr. Suggs, in an ironically affectionate tone of voice.

" I had it under my leg, thar, to make it on Bill, the first time it come trumps," was the ready reply.

" What's trumps?" asked Mr. Suggs, with a view of arriving at the import of the word.

" Nothin' a'n't trumps *now,*" said Simon, who misapprehended his father's meaning—" but *clubs* was, when you come along and busted up the game."

A part of this answer was Greek to the Reverend Mr. Suggs, but a portion of it was full of meaning.

They had then, most unquestionably, been "throwing" cards, the scoundrels! the "oudacious" little hellions!

"To the 'mulberry' with both on ye, in a hurry," said the old man sternly. But the lads were not disposed to be in a "hurry," for "the mulberry" was the scene of all formal punishment administered during work hours in the field. Simon followed his father, however, but made, as he went along, all manner of "faces" at the old man's back; gesticulated as if he were going to strike him between the shoulders with his fists, and kicking at him so as almost to touch his coat tail with his shoe. In this style they walked on to the mulberry tree, in whose shade Simon's brother Ben was resting. Of what transpired there, we shall speak in the next chapter.

CHAPTER THE SECOND.

SIMON GETS A "SOFT SNAP" OUT OF HIS DADDY.

IT must not be supposed that, during the walk to the place of punishment, Simon's mind was either inactive, or engaged in suggesting the grimaces and contortions wherewith he was pantomimically expressing his irreverent sentiments toward his father. Far from it. The movements of his limbs and features were the mere workings of habit—the self-grinding of the corporeal machine—for which his reasoning half was only remotely responsible. For while Simon's person was thus, on its own account, "making game" of old Jed'diah, his wits, in view of the anticipated flogging, were dashing, springing, bounding, darting about, in hot chase of some expedient suitable to the necessities of the case; much after the manner in which puss—when Betty, armed with the broom, and hotly seeking vengeance for pantry robbed or bed defiled, has closed upon her the garret doors and windows—attempts all sorts of impossible exits, to come down at last in the corner, with panting side and glaring eye, exhausted and defenceless. Our unfortunate hero could devise nothing by which he could reasonably expect to escape the heavy blows of his father. Having arrived at this conclusion and the "mulberry" about the same time, he stood with a dogged look awaiting the issue.

The old man Suggs made no remark to any one

while he was seizing up Bill—a process which, though
by no means novel to Simon, seemed to excite in him
a sort of painful interest.   He watched it closely, as
if endeavouring to learn the precise fashion of his father's knot; and when at last Bill was swung up
a-tiptoe to a limb, and the whipping commenced,
Simon's eye followed every movement of his father's
arm; and as each blow descended upon the bare
shoulders of his sable friend, his own body writhed
and " wriggled" in involuntary sympathy.

"It's the devil—it's hell," said Simon to himself,
" to take such a walloppin' as that.   Why the old
man looks like he wants to git to' the holler, if he
could—rot his old picter!   It's wuth, at the least, fifty
cents—je-e-miny how that hurt!—yes, it's wuth
three-quarters of a dollar to take that 'ere lickin'!
Wonder if I'm " predestinated," as old Jed'diah says,
to git the feller to it?   Lord, how daddy blows!   I
do wish to God he'd bust wide open, the durned old
deer-face!   If 'twa'n't for Ben helpin' him, I b'lieve
I'd give the old dog a tussel when it comes to my
turn.   It couldn't make the thing no wuss, if it didn't
make it no better.   'D rot it! what do boys have dad-
dies for, any how?   'Taint for nuthin' but jist to beat
'em and work 'em.—There's some use in mammies
—I kin poke my finger right in the old 'oman's eye,
and keep it thar, and if I say it aint thar, she'll say
so too.   I wish she was here to hold daddy off.   If
't,.a'n't so fur, I'd holler for her, any how.   How
she would cling to the old fellow's coat tail!"

Mr. Jedediah Suggs let down Bill and untied him.
Approaching Simon, whose coat was off, " Come,

Simon, son," said he, " cross them hands ; I'm gwine
to correct you."

" It aint no use, daddy," said Simon.

" Why so, Simon ?"

" Jist bekase it aint. I'm gwine to play cards as
long as I live. When I go off to myself, I'm gwine
to make my livin' by it. So what's the use of beat-
in' me about it ?"

Old Mr. Suggs groaned, as he was wont to do in
the pulpit, at this display of Simon's viciousness.

" Simon," said he, " you're a poor ignunt creetur.
You don't know nuthin', and you've never bin no
whars. If I was to turn you off, you'd starve in a
week—"

" I wish you'd try me," said Simon, " and jist see.
I'd win more money in a week than you can make in
a year. There ain't nobody round here kin make
seed corn off o' me at cards. I'm rale smart," he
added with great emphasis.

" Simon ! Simon ! you poor unlettered fool. Don't
you know that all card-players, and chicken-fighters,
and horse-racers go to hell ? You crack-brained
creetur you. And don't you know that them that
plays cards always loses their money, and—"

" Who win's it all then, daddy ?" asked Simon.

" Shet your mouth, you imperdent, slack-jawed
dog. Your daddy's a-tryin' to give you some good
advice, and you a-pickin' up his words that way. I
knowed a young man once, when I lived in Ogle-
tharp, as went down to Augusty and sold a hundred
dollars worth of cotton for his daddy, and some o'
them gambollers got him to drinkin', and the *very*

first night he was with 'em they got every cent of his money."

"They couldn't get my money in a *week*," said Simon. "Any body can git these here green feller's money; them's the sort I'm a-gwine to watch for myself. Here's what kin fix the papers jist about as nice as any body."

"Well, it's no use to argify about the matter," said old Jed'diah; "What saith the Scriptur'? 'He that begetteth a fool, doeth it to his sorrow.' Hence, Simon, you're a poor, misubble fool—so cross your hands!"

"You'd jist as well not, daddy; I tell you I'm gwine to follow playin' cards for a livin', and what's the use o' bangin' a feller about it? I'm as smart as any of 'em, and Bob Smith says them Augusty fellers can't make rent off o' me."

The reverend Mr. Suggs had once in his life gone to Augusta; an extent of travel which in those days was a little unusual. His consideration among his neighbours was considerably increased by the circumstance, as he had all the benefit of the popular inference, that no man could visit the city of Augusta without acquiring a vast superiority over all his untravelled neighbours, in every department of human knowledge. Mr. Suggs then, very naturally, felt ineffably indignant that an individual who had never seen any collection of human habitations larger than a log-house village—an individual, in short, no other or better than Bob Smith, should venture to express an opinion concerning the manners, customs, or any thing else appertaining to, or in any wise connected with, the *ultima Thule* of back-woods Georgians. There were two propositions which witnessed their own truth to the mind of Mr. Suggs—the one was, that a man who had never been at Augusta, could not know any thing about that city, or any place, or any thing else; the other, that one who *had* been there must, of necessity, be not only well informed as to all things connected with the city itself, but perfectly *au fait* upon all subjects whatsoever. It was, therefore, in a tone of mingled indignation and contempt that he replied to the last remark of Simon.

"*Bob Smith* says, does he? And who's *Bob Smith?* Much does *Bob Smith* know about Augusty! he's *been thar*, I reckon! Slipped off yerly some mornin', when nobody warn't noticin', and got back afore night! It's *only* a hundred and fifty mile. Oh, yes, *Bob Smith* knows *all* about it! *I* don't know nothin' about it! *I* a'n't never been to Augusty— *I* couldn't find the road thar, I reckon—ha! ha! *Bob—Smi—th!* The eternal stink! if he was only to see one o' them fine gentlemen in Augusty, with his fine broad-cloth, and bell-crown hat, and shoe-boots a-shinin' like silver, he'd take to the woods and kill himself a-runnin'. Bob Smith! that's whar all your devilment comes from, Simon."

"Bob Smith's as good as any body else, I judge; and a heap smarter than some. He showed me how to cut Jack," continued Simon, "and that's more nor some people can do, if they *have* been to Augusty."

"If Bob Smith kin do it," said the old man, "I kin too. I don't know it by that name; but if it's book knowledge or plain sense, and Bob kin do it, it's reasonable to s'pose that old Jed'diah Suggs won't be bothered bad. Is it any ways similyar to the rule of three, Simon?"

"Pretty much, daddy, but not adzactly," said Simon, drawing a pack from his pocket, to explain. "Now daddy," he proceeded, "you see these here four cards is what we calls the Jacks. Well, now the idee is, if you'll take the pack and mix 'em all up together, I'll take off a passel from top, and the bottom one of them I take off will be one of the Jacks."

"Me to mix 'em fust?" said old Jed'diah.

"Yes."

"And you not to see but the back of the top one, when you go to 'cut,' as you call it?"

"Jist so, daddy."

"And the backs all jist as like as kin be?" said the senior Suggs, examining the cards.

"More alike nor cow-peas," said Simon.

"It can't be done, Simon," observed the old man, with great solemnity.

"Bob Smith kin do it, and so kin I."

"It's agin nater, Simon; thar a'n't a man in Augusty, nor on top of the yeath that kin do it!"

"Daddy," said our hero, "ef you'll bet me——"

"What!" thundered old Mr. Suggs. "*Bet*, did you say?" and he came down with a *scorer* across Sim a's shoulders—"me, Jed'diah Suggs, that's been in the Lord's sarvice these twenty years—*me* bet, you nasty, sassy, triflin' ugly—"

"I didn't go to say *that* daddy; that warn't what I meant, adzactly. I went to say that ef you'd let me off from this here maulin' you owe me, and *give me* 'Bunch,' ef I cut Jack; I'd *give you* all this here silver, ef I didn't—that's all. To be sure, I allers knowed *you* wouldn't *bet*."

Old Mr. Suggs ascertained the exact amount of the silver which his son handed him, in an old leathern pouch, for inspection. He also, mentally, compared that sum with an imaginary one, the supposed value of a certain Indian poney, called "Bunch," which he had bought for his "old woman's" Sunday riding, and which had sent the old lady into a fence corner, the first and only time she ever mounted him. As he weighed the pouch of silver in his hand, Mr. Suggs also endeavoured to analyse the character of the transaction proposed by Simon. "It sartinly *can't* be nothin' but *givin'*, no way it kin be twisted," he murmured to himself. "I *know* he can't do it, so there's no resk. What makes bettin'? The resk. It's a one-sided business, and I'll jist let him give me all his money, and that'll put all his wild sportin' notions out of his head."

"Will you stand it, daddy?" asked Simon, by way of waking the old man up. "You mought as well, for the whippin' won't do you no good, and as for Bunch, nobody about the plantation won't ride him but me."

"Simon," replied the old man, "I agree to it. Your old daddy is in a close place about payin' for his land; and this here money—it's jist eleven dollars, lacking of twenty-five cents—will help out mightily. But mind, Simon, ef any thing's said

C

about this, herearter, remember, you *give* me the money."

"Very well, daddy, and ef the thing works up instid o' down, I s'pose we'll say you give *me* Bunch —eh?'"

"You won't never be troubled to tell how you come by Bunch; the thing's agin nater, and can't be done. What old Jed'diah Suggs knows, he knows as good as any body. Give me them fixments, Simon."

Our hero handed the cards to his father, who, dropping the plough-line with which he had intended to tie Simon's hands, turned his back to that individual, in order to prevent his witnessing the operation of *mixing*. He then sat down, and very leisurely commenced shuffling the cards, making, however, an exceedingly awkward job of it. Restive *kings* and *queens* jumped from his hands, or obstinately refused to slide into the company of the rest of the pack. Occasionally a sprightly *knave* would insist on *facing* his neighbour; or, pressing his edge against another's, half double himself up, and then skip away. But Elder Jed'diah perseveringly continued his attempts to subdue the refractory, while heavy drops burst from his forehead, and ran down his cheeks. All of a sudden an idea, quick and penetrating as a rifle-ball, seemed to have entered the cranium of the old man. He chuckled audibly. The devil had suggested to Mr. Suggs an *impromptu* "stock," which would place the chances of Simon, already sufficiently slim, in the old man's opinion, without the range of possibility. Mr. Suggs forthwith proceeded to cull out all the *picter ones*, so as to be certain to include the *Jacks*, and place them at the bottom; with the evident intention of keeping Simon's fingers above these when he should cut. Our hero, who was quietly looking over his father's shoulders all the time, did not seem alarmed by this disposition of the cards; on the contrary, he smiled as if he felt perfectly confident of success, in spite of it.

"Now, daddy," said Simon, when his father had announced himself ready, "narry one of us aint got to look at the cards, while I'm a cuttin'; if we do, it'll spile the conjuration."

"Very well."

"And another thing—you've got to look me right dead in the eye, daddy—will you?"

"To be sure—to be sure;" said Mr. Suggs; "fire away."

Simon walked up close to his father, and placed his hand on the pack. Old Mr. Suggs looked in Simon's eye, and Simon returned the look for about three seconds, during which a close observer might have detected a suspicious working of the wrist of the hand on the cards, but the elder Suggs did not remark it.

"Wake snakes! day's a-breakin'! Rise Jack!" said Simon, cutting half a dozen cards from the top of the pack, and presenting the face of the bottom one for the inspection of his father.

It was the Jack of hearts!

Old Mr. Suggs staggered back several steps with uplifted eyes and hands!

"Marciful master!" he exclaimed, "ef the boy

haint! well, how in the round creation of the —— !
Ben, did you ever? to be sure and sartin, Satan has
power on this yeath!" and Mr. Suggs groaned in very
bitterness.

"You never seed nothin' like that in *Augusty*, did
ye, daddy?" asked Simon, with a malicious wink at
Ben.

"Simon, how *did* you do it? queried the old man,
without noticing his son's question.

"Do it daddy? Do it? 'Taint nothin'. I done
it jist as easy as—shootin'."

Whether this explanation was entirely, or in any
degree, satisfactory to the perplexed mind of Elder
Jed'diah Suggs, cannot, after the lapse of time which
has intervened, be sufficiently ascertained. It is certain, however, that he pressed the investigation no
farther, but merely requested his son Benjamin to
witness the fact, that in consideration of his love and
affection for his son Simon, and in order to furnish
the donee with the means of leaving that portion of
the state of Georgia, he bestowed upon him the im-
practicable poney, "Bunch."

"Jist so, daddy; jist so; I'll witness that. But it
'minds me mightily of the way mammy *give* old
Trailler the side of bacon, last week. She a-sweep-
in' up the hath; the meat on the table—old Trailler
jumps up, gethers the bacon and darts! mammy arter
him with the broom-stick, as fur as the door—but
seein' the dog has got the start, she shakes the stick
at him and hollers, 'You sassy, aig-sukkin', roguish,
gnatty, flop-eared varmint! take it along! take it
along! I only wish 'twas full of a'snic, and ox-vo-

mit, and blue vitrul, so as 'twould cut your interls into chitlins!' That's about the way you give Bunch to Simon."

"Oh, shuh! Ben," remarked Simon, "I wouldn't run on that way; daddy couldn't help it, it was *predestinated*—'whom he hath, he will,' you know;" and the rascal pulled down the under lid of his left eye at his brother. Then addressing his father, he asked, "Warn't it, daddy?"

"To be sure—to be sure—all fixed aforehand," was old Mr. Suggs' reply.

"Didn't I tell you so, Ben?" said Simon—"*I* knowed it was all fixed aforehand;" and he laughed until he was purple in the face.

"What's in ye? What are ye laughin' about?" asked the old man wrothily.

"Oh, it's so funny that it could all a' been *fixed aforehand!*" said Simon, and laughed louder than before.

The obtusity of the Reverend Mr. Suggs, however, prevented his making any discoveries. He fell into a brow study, and no further allusion was made to the matter.

It was evident to our hero that his father intended he should remain but one more night beneath the paternal roof. What mattered it to Simon?

He went home at night, curried and fed Bunch; whispered confidentially in his ear that he was the "fastest piece of hoss-flesh, accordin' to size, that ever shaded the yeath;" and then busied himself in preparing for an early start on the morrow.

CHAPTER THE THIRD.

SIMON SPECULATES.

OLD Mrs. Suggs' big red rooster had hardly ceased crowing in announcement of the coming dawn, when Simon mounted the intractable Bunch. Both were in high spirits—our hero at the idea of unrestrained license in future; and Bunch from a mesmerical transmission to himself of a portion of his master's deviltry. Simon raised himself in the stirrups, yelled a tolerably fair imitation of the Creek war-whoop, and shouted—

"I'm off, old stud! remember the Jack-a-hearts!"

Bunch shook his little head, tucked down his tail, ran side-ways, as if going to fall; and then suddenly reared, squealed, and struck off at a brisk gallop.

Out of sight of his old home, Simon became serious—half melancholy. He thought over all the little incidents of his life—of his frolics with Bill and Ben —of the neighbour boys and girls—of the doting love of his mother; and he couldn't deny to himself, that it was sad to leave them all thus, perhaps no more to return to them. How long he may have indulged these sombre reflections is unknown; they were at length interrupted however, by an outburst of laughter, so sudden and violent that Bunch almost jumped out of his hide in a paroxysm of fright.

" Now won't it be great!" said he, thinking aloud. " Won't the old 'oman jump, and sputter, and tear

off her cap, and break her spectacles!" and Simon
roared with delight at the fun visible to his mind's
eye. "And Jee-e-hu!" he continued, "won't old
Jed'diah grunt, and cuss, and pray! I think I see
him now, with his shirt tail a-flyin'! Hoop-ee! *won't*
they roll over the floor, and have chicken fits, a
dozen at a time! And thar's Ben, 'd rot him, 'ill
have every bit of fun to hisself! But I don't care no
how; I know adzactly how 'twill be—thar *she* lays
a-kickin', and thar *hit* is, on the hath, busted all to
flinderjigs; and thar's daddy, a flyin' round, a-turnin'
over every thing, jest as ef he had the blind-staggers.
And bime-by, she'll sort o' come too, and daddy'll
ax her ef she's bad hurt; and then right away she'll
take another one o' them starricks, and then from
that, of all the kickin', snortin', hollerin', *and* cavor-
tin' that ever was seen, they'll do it—haw! haw!
haw!"

This quick transition from gloomy feelings to furious mirth, would perhaps be inexplicable to our readers, unless we mentioned the fact that Simon had, as
soon as he arose, stolen into his mother's room, and
nicely loaded the old lady's pipe with a thimble full
of gunpowder; neatly covering the "villainous salt-
petre" with tobacco. It was the scene he thought
likely to occur when Mrs. Suggs should begin to so-
lace herself with her matutinal "smoke," which made
him laugh so loudly and so long. Whether the explosion did actually occur, must ever remain a question of some doubt: but there certainly is great plau-
sibility in Simon's view of the matter, which is, that
every thing was so excellently arranged, that he'll

"be damned if it didn't blow the old woman within a foot, or a foot and a half of kingdom come." Howbeit, there are those who do not scruple to declare their belief that Mr. Suggs hazards nothing by such an asserveration—seeing, as they declare, that the probability of his escaping the clutches of the old gentleman with the cloven hoof is exceedingly minute, independent of any mistake in relation to the explosion of the pipe. On this point, *we*, of course, have nothing to say. We are Captain Suggs' biographer. If he be saved, well! If not, it's none of our business. On so delicate a question, propriety will barely allow us the single remark, that should the Captain fail to slip past St. Peter, none but the "duly qualified" need thereafter attempt to effect an entrance.

His fit of laughter over, it was not long before Simon was at Bob Smith's grocery; and here, we are sorry to say, we lose all trace—at least all authentic trace—of him, for the next twenty years. Over, and over again, we have questioned "those who ought to know," but without ever having been able to get our hero one foot beyond the grocery. Like a sulky mule, there he stops every time, at Bob Smith's grocery. And in truth, we can say that the habit of stopping at places of that description has only been confirmed by time; notwithstanding which, however, it is right we should add, that we have never known the Captain to remain at one longer than six weeks at any one visit—a period of time greatly less than twenty years. We therefore do not, for a moment, entertain the idea that the Captain remained at Bob Smith's during the last-mentioned period. The supposition is altogether improbable: Bob Smith himself, did not, in all likelihood, remain there so long. But so it is, all concur that he went there, while none know how long he remained, or whither he afterwards went. Some *have heard* that he went thence to Augusta; others aver that *in their opinion*, he travelled away down into the low country " whar they call sop, *gravy;* again, some say that a man very much like him was seen travelling in the Cherokee country; and not a few contend that he married, and settled in an adjoining eastern county, leading a quiet and blameless life for many years. It is certain that he married: eight or ten strapping boys attest that fact—the rest is all doubt, uncertainty, and vague speculation. But, asks the reader, cannot Captain Suggs himself solve this mystery? Softly, good friend! The Captain chooses to be silent on the subject, and it does not become his friends to press him with questions. We once knew an individual in whose history there was a *hiatus* of four years. Of all other portions of his life he spoke with the utmost freedom, but to these four years he never referred, and when questioned closely as to how he spent them, his reply was ever a wink, and " None of your business, sir!" Some years after his death, it was accidentally discovered that the four years inaccounted for were spent in a penitentiary. Now we, by no means, mean to insinuate any thing like this in regard to Captain Suggs. Penitentiaries might gape on every side, and we'd give long odds that the Captain would be found outside while any body else was! We *but mean to intimate* that the Captain has some

very good reason for not referring in any way to the
unilluminated period, or any events which may have
transpired therein.   It' a free country, this, and no
man is obliged by the law—and if the law do not
oblige him, who or what else shall?—to state to the
public where he lived, or how he spent his time, during any particular year or series of years. Suppose—
we speak hypothetically—some enemy of Captain
Suggs were to assert, that during the twenty years he
was "buried to the world," he had lived in the
county of Carroll, in the "sovereignty" of Georgia,
where, from "time immemorial," the chief occupation
of the inhabitants has been to steal horses—Carroll,
the head-quarters of the old "Pony Club!" Just
suppose that!   And suppose further, that this bold
and knowing individual should accompany that asser-
tion with a wink of the eye, or a down-drawing of
his mouth corners, or the placing of his thumb on the
tip of his nose, or any other gesture or gesticulation
intended to express covertly, (and falsely, of course,)
the charge that Captain Suggs himself had stolen
horses! What would the world—what would we
say? It might, perhaps, be presumptuous in us to
give a supposititious answer for the world ; but for ourself we can speak outright. WE should say—boldly,
haughtily, indignantly say—"LET HIM PROVE IT !"

Skipping over a score of years, then, during which
the Captain's head from close application to theologi-
cal studies, or some other cause, had become quite
gray, we find him, in the year of our Lord 1833,
snugly settled on public land on the Tallapoosa river,
in the midst of that highly respectable town of Indians,

known as the Oakfuskees.   There he was, as jolly as
Bacchus, with a pretty large family and considerable
experience, but without funds—a speculator in Creek
lands!

To the uninitiated it may seem odd that a man
without a dollar should be a land speculator.   We
admit that there is a seeming incongruity in the idea:
but have those in whose minds speculation and capital are inseparably connected, ever heard of a process
by which lands were sold, deeds executed, and all
that sort of thing completely arranged, and all without once troubling the owner of the soil for an opinion
even, in regard to the matter?   Yet such occurrences were frequent some years since, in this
country, and they illustrated *one* mode of speculation
requiring little, if any, cash capital.   But there were
other modes of speculating without money or credit;
and Captain Simon Suggs became as familiar with
every one of them, as with the way to his own corn-
crib.   As for those branches of the business requiring
actual pecuniary outlay, he regarded them as only fit
to be pursued by purse-proud clod-heads.   Any fool,
he reasoned, could speculate if he had money.   But
to buy, to sell, to make profits, without a cent in one's
pocket—this required judgment, discretion, ingenuity—in short, genius!

The following is a true account of the Captain's
first "operation:"

Shortly after the land office had been opened at
Montgomery, a perfect mania for entering government
lands prevailed through the country.   Speculators
from Georgia and Tennessee, and from the older set-

tlements of this state, might be seen dashing along at
half-speed, almost any hour in the twenty-four, towards Montgomery.   Many a long and hard race was
run by rival land-hunters, intent upon the acquisition
of the same " first-rate eighty" or " tip-top quarter."
Ah! but those were " the times that tried" horse-
flesh!   But as we were going to say, there was a
public house on the road from Captain Suggs' neighbourhood to Wetumpka, about fifteen miles from the
latter place, and double that distance from Montgomery.   At this house the Captain stopped once, in
the hope of finding prey among the numerous speculators who thronged it almost every night, going to,
or returning from, the land office.   It so chanced on
the occasion to which we refer, that supper-time
brought with it no additional guest to Mr. Doublejoy's table; and the Captain having nothing better to
do, retired early to bed.   He had hardly fixed himself snugly between the sheets, however, when two
persons rode up to the house, almost simultaneously,
and put up for the night.   One of these persons came
from the direction of Wetumpka, the other from the
Georgia end of the road.   It was not long before the
new-comers, who proved to be old acquaintances,
had dispatched supper, and taken a bed together in
a room adjoining the Captain's.   Their bed, however, was close to his, and the cracks of the log par-
tition enabled him to catch a part of the conversation
which occurred after the strangers had lain down.
From it he gathered the facts, that one of the parties
was bound for Montgomery, and that his object was
to enter a tract of land, upon which was a very valu-

able mill-shoal. He listened to hear the numbers, but the speculator only incidentally mentioned that it was part of section ten, leaving the Captain entirely in the dark as to the township and range.

"If," muttered he, " I could only get the township and range, I'd make a *cahoot* business with old man Doublejoy, get the money from him, and enter that mill-shoal with the twenty foot fall, before ten o'clock to-morrow." But though he listened closely, he could obtain no more accurate description of the land than that it was a part of section ten, in the eastern part of his own county, near Dodd's store, and valuable as a location for a set of mills. He learned further, that the stranger was very apprehensive that an agent of a certain company would be at his heels by morning, and give him a race for the land. This determined the captain how to act, and he rolled over and went to sleep.

By day-break the next morning the mill-shoal man was off. The Captain was " wide awake," but said nothing until his intended victim was fairly gone. He then ordered his own horse and dashed down the road at half-speed. By the time he had ridden half a mile, he overtook the land-seeker, whose horse seemed very stiff and slightly lame.

"—Mornin', mister," was the Captain's salutation, as he rode up by the stranger's side. " Sorter airish this morning'—judge that horse o' yourn is tetched with the founder."

"I'm afraid so," was the reply.

"Oh, I'll be damned if you need be *afeerd* of it, mister. It's jest so," said Captain Suggs. " In two hours more he won't be able to step over the butt cut of a broom straw."

"I hate it worse," said the stranger, "because I'm just now in a particular hurry to get to Montgomery on important business. I would give any gentleman," he continued, eyeing the Captain's old sorrel, "an excellent trade, to get a nag that would do a few hours' hard travel."

"Oh, I understand—but you needn't view this here old animal like you thought so much on him. I tell you what, mister ——, what did you say your name happened to be? Jones, eh?—well, 'squire Jones, I'll tell you on the honor of a gentleman, if you was to 'light from your horse and lay the purtiest hunderd dollar bill that ever had a picter on it, across your saddle, I wouldn't take 'em both for old Ball at this particular time. In four hours I must be in Montgomery."

"You certainly must be going to enter land, from your hurry."

"A body would think so, that looked into the matter rightly. And what's more," said the Captain, "it's quite likely there's somebody else after my land from what I've hearn—so I must push. Good mornin'."

As the Captain struck his heels against Ball's sides, Mr. Jones seemed to grow nervous.

"Whereabouts does your land lie?" he asked.

"Up in Tallapoosy," replied Suggs; and again he thumped Ball with his heels.

Mr. Jones evidently grew more uneasy.—"What part of the county?" he asked.

"Close to the Chambers' line—not far from Dodd's store—get along Ball!" was the Captain's answer.

"Stop, sir—if you please—perhaps—I would like —we'd better perhaps under—" gasped Mr. Jones in great agitation.

"To be sure we had," said Suggs, with great *sang froid*. "It's jist as you say. But what the devil's the matter with you?—are you goin' to take a fit?"

Jones explained that he thought it likely they were both going to enter the same piece of land. "What did you say was the numbers of yours?" he asked.

"I didn't mention *no* numbers as well as I *now* recollect," said Suggs with a bland smile. "Hows'-ever, 'squire Jones, as it looks like your gear don't fit you somehow, I'll jist tell you that the land I'm after is a d—d little, no-account quarter section, that nobody would have but me; its poor and piney, but it's got a snug little shoal on it, with twenty or twen-ty-five foot fall, and maybe they'll want to build a little town at Dodd's some of these days, and I mought sell 'em the lumber. Seein' you're pretty much afoot even if you wanted it, I may as well give you the numbers, if I can without lookin' in my pocket book. It's ten—ten—ten—Section ten, Township—Oh, damn the number, I never can remember—"

"S. E. quarter of 10: 22, 25—aint it?" asked Jones, who looked perfectly wild.

"Now you hit me!—good as four aces—them's the figures!" said Captain Suggs.

"It's the same piece I'm after; I'll give you fifty dollars to let me enter it."

"You wouldn't now, would you?"

" I'll give you a hundred!"

" Try again!"

" Well, I'll give you a hundred and fifty, and not
a dollar more," said Jones in a decisive tone.

" Let's see—well, I reckon—tho' I don't know—
yes, I suppose I must let you have it, as I can't well
spar' the money to enter it at this time, no how"—
remarked Suggs, with much truth, as his cash on
hand didn't amount to quite one-fortieth part of the
sum necessary to make the entry. "But we must
swap horses, and you must give me twenty dollars
boot."

This was agreed to, and Captain Simon Suggs received the one hundred and seventy dollars with the
air of a man who was conferring a most substantial
favour; and made divers remarks laudatory of his own
disposition while Mr. Jones counted the bills and
changed the saddles. "Give my respects to Colonel
Benson when you see him at the land office; tell him
we're all well"—said he to Jones as they shook
hands. Certes, he didn't know Colonel Benson from
the great chief of the Pawnees: but Suggs has his
weaknesses like other people.

Turning his horse's head homeward, Captain Suggs
soliloquized somewhat in this vein: " A pretty, toloble fair mornin's work, I should say. A hundred
and seventy dollars in the clear spizarinctum, and a
horse wuth jist fifty dollars more than old Ball!—
That makes about two hundred and twenty dollars,
as nigh as I can guess without I had Dolbear along!
Now some fellers, after makin' sich a little decent rise
would milk the cow dry, by pushin' on to Double-

joy's, startin' a runner the nigh way to Montgomery, by the Augusty ferry, and enterin' that land in somebody else's name before Jones gits thar! But honesty's the best policy. Honesty's the bright spot in *any* man's character!—Fair play's a jewel, but honesty beats it all to pieces! Ah yes, *honesty*, HONESTY's the stake that Simon Suggs will ALLERS tie to! What's a man without his inteegerty?"

CHAPTER THE FOURTH.

SIMON STARTS FORTH TO FIGHT THE "TIGER," AND
FALLS IN WITH A CANDIDATE WHOM HE "DOES" TO
A CRACKLIN'.

READER! didst ever encounter the Tiger?—not the
bounding creature of the woods, with deadly fang and
mutilating claw, that preys upon blood and muscle—
but the stealthier and more ferocious animal which
ranges amid "the busy haunts of men"—which feeds
upon coin and bank-notes—whose spots, more attrac-
tive than those of its namesake of the forest, dazzle
and lure, like the brilliantly varying hues of the
charmer snake, the more intensely and irresistibly, the
longer they are looked upon—the thing, in short, of
pasteboard and ivory, mother-of-pearl and mahogany
—THE FARO BANK!

Take a look at the elegant man dealing out the
cards, from that *bijou* of a box, there. Observe with
what graceful dexterity he manages all the appliances
of his art! The cards seem to leap forth rather in
obedience to his will, than to be pulled out by his
fingers. As he throws them in alternate piles, note
the whiteness and symmetry of his hand, the snowy
spotlessness of the linen exposed by the turn-up of
his coat-cuff, and the lustre of the gem upon his little
finger. Now look in his face. Isn't he a handsome
fellow—a man to make hearts feminine ache? And
how singularly at variance with the exciting nature

of his occupation, is the expression of his countenance! How placid! He has hundreds depending
upon the turn of the next card, and yet his face is
entirely calm, if you except a very slight twitching
of the eye-lids, which are so nearly closed that the
long lashes nearly intermingle. A pretty, gentlemanly
Tiger-keeper, in sooth! He smiles now—mark the
beauty of that large mouth, and the dazzling splen-
dour of those teeth!—as he addresses the florid and
flushed young man, there at the table, whose last dollar he has just swept from the board. "The bank
is singularly fortunate to-night. Nothing but the best
sort of luck could have saved it from the skilful com-
bination with which you attacked. Ninety-nine times
out of a hundred you would have broken it—I've
had an escape." Spite of his ruinous losses, the poor
devil is flattered by the compliment. Oh ass! of
skull most impenetrable! To-day you are, or rather
you were, on your way to college, with the first year's
expenses—the close parings of the comforts of the
old widow your mother, and the thin, blue-eyed girl
your sister—in your pocket. This day twelvemonth,
you will keep the scores of a gambling house and
live upon the perquisites! See if you don't! The
Tiger has cheated the professors, and you have
cheated your family and—yourself!

Almost every man has his idiosyncrasy—his pet
and peculiar opinion on some particular subject.
Captain Simon Suggs has his; and he clings to it with
a pertinacity that defies, alike the suggestions of reason, and the demonstrations of experience. Simon
believes that he CAN WHIP THE TIGER, A FAIR FIGHT.

He *has* always believed it; he *will* always believe it.
The idea has obtained a lodgment in his cranium and
peremptorily refuses to be ejected! It is the weak
point—the *Achilles' heel,* as one might say—of his
character. Remind him of the time, in Montgomery,
when by a bite of this same Tiger, he lost his money
and horse, and was compelled to trudge home afoot!
ah, but *then,* he "hadn't got the hang of the game."
Bring to his recollection how severely it scratched
him in Girard!—oh, but "*that* fellow rung in a two-
card box" upon him. Ask him if he did'nt drop a
couple of hundreds at the Big Council? Certainly--
but *then* he was "drinky and played careless;" and
so on to the end.—Still he inflexibly believes he is to
get the upper hand of the Tiger, some day when it
is exceedingly fat, and wear its hide as a trophy!
Still the invincible beast lacerates him instead! Such
is the infatuation of Captain Suggs.

Acting under this delusion Simon determined, as
soon as he obtained the money by the "land transaction" recorded in our last, to visit the city of Tus-
caloosa, where the Legislature was to commence its
session in a few days, with the double object of
"weeding out" members, and making a grand de-
monstration against some bank. His "pile," to be
sure, considering how extensive were the operations
contemplated, was certainly small—inadequate. But
as Simon remarked, upon setting out, "there is no
telling which way luck or a half-broke steer will run."
So perhaps the amount of his capital was really not a
matter of any great consequence. He carried a hundred and fifty dollars with him; the results might not

have been different, had he carried a thousand and fifty—who shall say?

The Captain—would that we could avoid the anachronism we commit every time we apply the military designation of Simon, in speaking of events which occurred anterior to the year of grace 1836;—however, let it go—the Captain left his horse at a farm-house near Montgomery, and took the mail-coach for the capital. The only other passenger was a gentleman who was about to visit the seat of government, with the intention of making himself a bank director, as speedily as possible. The individual assumed, and insisted on believing, that Simon was the member from Tallapoosa. This, of course Simon denied—but denied " in such a sort!"——

" I should be highly pleased, sir, if you could make it consistent with your views of the public good, to receive your support for that directorship, sir"— quoth the candidate.

" What keen people you candidates are, to find out folks," said Simon. " But mind, I haint said yet I was a member. I told wife when I started, I warn't goin' to tell nobod——hello! I liked to a ketcht myself—didn't I ?" said Simon, winking pleasantly at the embryo director.

" Ah, you're a close, prudent fellow, I see," said the candidate; " I like prudence, sir, in public officers, sir! It's the bulwark, sir, to hang the anchor of the state upon, to speak nautically, sir. But as I was remarking, if duty to the state, to the country, and to the institution itself, would permit, I would be profoundly grate——."

"Yes"—interrupted Suggs—"prudence is the stob I fasten the grape-vine of *my* cunnoo to. I said I wouldn't tell it—nor I won't."

"The present directory, sir, or at least a portion of it, sir, does not display that zeal, sir, in the service of the public—that promptitude, sir, and that spirit of accommodation—which the community has a right to expect, sir. Though, perhaps, I oughtn't, on account of the delicacy of my position, to make invidious remarks, sir—and sir, I make it a point never to do so—still, I may be permitted to say, that should the legislature honor *me* with their confidence, sir, I shall—that is to say, sir, a very different state of affairs may be anticipated. The institution, sir, should command the whole of my intellectual energies and faculties, sir. The institution, sir——."

"To be sure! to be sure! I onderstand," said Simon. "The institution's what we're all after. As for the present directory, they're all a pack of d—d swell-heads. Afore I left Montgomery I went to one on 'em, and told him who I was, and let on that I wanted a few dollars to pay expenses down. He knowed, in course, I'd soon be gittin' four——hello! I'm about to ketch mysel' agin!"—and Simon laughed, and winked at his companion.

"Four dollars *per diem*, besides mileage," said the candidate with a witching smile.

"Never mind about that, I say nothin' myself—other people can say what they please. Any how, that feller wouldn't let me have a dollar!"

"What ungentlemanly conduct!" remarked the financier, energetically.

"D—d if he would—not a dollar—without I'd pledge myself to support him. *That* sir, I scorned to do," continued Simon, half rising from his seat, and swelling with indignation; "so I told him I'd see him as deep in h–ll as a pigeon could fly in a fortnight, first———"

"A very proper reply, sir—a very spirited reply, sir—just such a one, sir, as a man of high moral principle, refined feelings, pure patrio———"

"Oh, I gin him thunder and lightnin' stewed down to a strong pison, I tell you. I cussed him up one side and down tother, twell thar warn't the bigness of your thumb nail, that warn't *properly* cussed. And in the windin' up, I told him I'd pay my stage fare as fur towards Tuskalusy as my money hilt out, and walk the rest of the way, I would—but I'll show him," added the captain with a savage frown.

"Magnanimous, sir! that was magnanimous! A great moral spectacle, sir! You cursing the director, sir—withering him up with virtuous indignation—threatening to walk eighty miles, sir, over very inferior roads, to discharge your public functions—he cowering, as doubtless he did, before the representative of the people! Yes, sir, it was a sublime moral spectacle, worthy of a comparison with any recorded specimens of Roman or Spartan magnanimity, sir. How nobly did it vindicate the purity of the representative character, sir!"

"Belikes it did"—said the Captain—"shouldn't be surprised. There *was* smartly of a row betwixt us, certin. We did'nt make quite as much noise as a panter and a pack of hounds, but we made *some.*

When we blow'd off, I judge he had the wust of it:
he looked like he had, any how."

"No doubt of it, sir; no doubt at all, sir. And
now, my dear sir, if you will permit me to indicate
what would have been *my* deportment upon such an
occasion, I trust I can make you comprehend the dif-
ference between the conduct of an insolent official,
and that of the high-bred, gentlemanly, public func-
tionary!"

Captain Suggs gesticulated his willingness to listen;
felicitating himself the while, upon the fact that Mr.
Smith, his county member, would not be along for
several days. The chances were altogether favourable for making a "raise," without fear of *immediate*
detection—which is all the Captain ever cared for.
So he isn't taken red-handed, after-claps may go to
the devil!

"Why, sir," resumed the candidate, after taking
a sly peep at a printed list, to get the name of the
member from Tallapoosa—"why, sir, if you had approached *me* as you did the individual of whom we
have been speaking; I occupying—you understand,
sir—the important fiscal station of bank director, and
you the highly honorable official position which you
do occupy, of representative of the respectable county
of Talla—"

"Stop! I never said my name was Smith; nor I
never set myself up for a legislatur man! You heerd
me tell the driver when I got up, not to tell the people who I was and whar I was goin'!"

"Oh, *we* understand all that, my dear sir, perfectly—perfectly!" said the candidate, with a smile

of humorous intelligence.—" There are many reasons
why gentlemen of distinction should at times desire
to travel without being known."

" *I'll* be d—d if thar ain't !" thought Captain Simon
Suggs.

" But my dear sir, there are persons so skilled in
human nature, so acute in their perceptions of worth
and talent, that they detect at a glance those whom
the people have honored. You can't pass us my
dear sir!—ha! ha! Oh no! We recognize you at
once! However, as I was going on to remark—had
you approached me under the circumstances stated, I
should have said to you—Colonel Smith, your elec-
tion by the enlightened people of the important county
you represent, is ample guaranty to *me*, that you are
a gentleman of the nicest honor, and the most unim-
peachable veracity, even if the fact were not con-
clusively attested by your personal appearance. The
sum you need, my dear Colonel, for expenses, is of
course too small to justify a discount. Will you oblige me by drawing for the requisite amount on my
private funds?—that's what *I*, sir, should have said,
sir, under the circumstances."

" By the Lord, stranger," remarked the Captain,
seizing the candidate's hand and shaking it repeatedly
with great warmth, to all appearance as completely
overwhelmed with gratitude for the supposititious loan,
as he could possibly have been had it been real—
" by the Lord, that *would* a-been the way! I'd a'stuck
to a feller that done *that* way, twell the cows come
home—I'd cut the big vein of my neck before I'd
ever desert sich a friend! I'd wade to my ears in

blood, to fight by *that* man's side; d—d if I wouldn't."

" Perhaps," said the candidate, " it isn't too late *yet*, to offer you a trifling accommodation of the sort ?'"

" No, it aint too late at all," answered Simon with admirable *naiveté*; " I could take a twenty, to right smart advantage yet!"

The office-seeker's pocket book was out in a twinkling, and a bank note transferred therefrom to Suggs' vest pocket.

" Of course, without the slightest reference to this little transaction, my dear Colonel, I count on your help."

" Give us your hand," said Suggs between his sobs—for the disinterested generosity of his companion had moved him to weeping—and they shook hands with great cordiality.

" You'll use your influence with your senator and other friends ?"

" Look me in the eye!" replied the Captain with an almost tragic air.

The candidate looked steadily, for two seconds, in Simon's tearful eye.

" You see *honesty* thar—don't you ?"

" I do! I do!" said the candidate with emotion.

" That's sufficient, aint it ?"

" Most amply sufficient—most amply sufficient, my dear Colonel"—and then they shook hands again, and took a drink from the tickler which the financier carried in his carpet bag.

Suggs and his new friend travelled the remainder

of the way to Tuskaloosa, in excellent companion-
ship, as it was reasonable they should.   They told
their tales, sang their songs, and drank their liquor
like a jovial pair as they were—the candidate paying
all scores wherever they halted.   And so things went
pleasantly with Simon until his meeting with the
tiger, which ensued immediately upon his arrival, and
whereof we defer a description to the succeeding
chapter.

CHAPTER THE FIFTH.

SIMON FIGHTS "THE TIGER" AND GETS WHIPPED—BUT
COMES OUT NOT MUCH THE "WORSE FOR WEAR."

As a matter of course, the first thing that engaged
the attention of Captain Suggs upon his arrival in
Tuskaloosa, was his proposed attack upon his enemy.
Indeed, he scarcely allowed himself time to bolt,
without mastication, the excellent supper served to
him at Duffie's, ere he outsallied to engage the ad-
versary.   In the street, he suffered not himself to be
beguiled into a moment's loitering, even by the
strange sights which under other circumstances would
certainly have enchained his attention.   The windows
of the great drug store cast forth their blaze of varied
light in vain; the music of a fine amateur band preparing for a serenade, was no music for him; he
paused not in front of the bookseller's, to inspect the
prints, or the huge-lettered advertising cards.   In
short, so eager was he to give battle to the "Tiger,"
that the voice of the ring-master, as it came distinctly
into the street from the circus—the sharp joke of the
clown, and the perfectly-shadowed figures of "Dandy
Jack" and the other performers, whisking rapidly
round upon the canvass—failed to shake, in the
slightest degree, the resolute determination of the
courageous and indomitable Captain.

As he hurried along, however, with the long stride
of the back-woods, hardly turning his head, and to

all appearance, oblivious altogether of things exter-
nal, he held occasional "confabs" with himself in
regard to the unusual objects which surrounded him—
for Suggs is an observant man, and notes with much
accuracy whatever comes before him, all the while a
body would suppose him to be asleep, or in a "turkey dream" at least.   On the present occasion his
communings with himself commenced opposite the
window of the drug-store,—"Well, thar's the most
deffrunt sperrets in *that grocery* ever *I* seed!   Thar's
koniac, and old peach, and rectified, and lots I can't
tell thar names!   That light-yaller bottle tho', in the
corner thar, that's Tenne*see*!   I'd know that *any*
whar!   And that tother bottle's rot-gut, ef I know
myself—bit a drink, I reckon, as well's the rest!
What a power o' likker they do keep in this here
town; ef I warn't goin' to run agin the bank, I'd
sample some of it, too, I reether expect.   But it don't
do for a man to sperrets much when he's pursuin' the
beast—"

"H–ll and scissors! who ever seed the like of the
books!   Aint thar a pile!   Do wonder what sort of
a office them fellers in thar keeps, makes 'em want
so many!   They don't read 'em *all*, I judge!   Well,
mother-wit kin beat book-larnin, at *any* game!   Thar's
'squire Hadenskelt up home, he's got two cart-loads
of law books—tho' that's no tech to this feller's—and
here's what knocked a fifty outen him once, at short
cards, afore a right smart, active sheep could flop his
tail *ary* time; and kin do it agin, whenever he gits
over his shyness!   Human natur' and the human family is *my* books, and I've never seed many but

what I could hold my own with. Let me git one o' these book-larnt fellers over a bottle of "old corn," and a handful of the dokkyments, and I'm d—d apt to git what he knows, and in a ginral way gives *him* a wrinkle into the bargain! Books aint fitten for no-thin' but jist to give to childen goin' to school, to keep 'em outen mischief. As old Jed'diah used to say, book-larnin spiles a man ef he's got mother-wit, and ef he aint got that, it don't do him no good—"

" Hello agin! Here's a sirkis, and ef I warnt in a hurry, right here I'd drop a quarter, providin' I couldn't fix it to slip in for nothin', which is always the cheapest in a ginral way!"

Thus ruminating, Simon at length reached CLARE's. Passing into the bar-room, he stood a moment, look-ing around to ascertain the direction in which he should proceed to find the faro banks, which he had heard were nightly exhibited there. In a corner of the room he discovered a stair-way, above which was burning a lurid-red lamp. Waiting for no other in-dication, he strode up the stairs. At the landing-place above he found a door which was closed and locked, but light came through the key-hole, and the sharp rattling of dice and jingling of coin, spoke con-clusively of the employment of the occupants of the room.

Simon knocked.

" Hello!" said somebody within.

" Hello yourself!" said the Captain.

" What do you want?" said the voice from the room.

" A game," was the Captain's laconic answer.

" What's the name?" again inquired the person within.

" Cash," said Simon.

"He'll do," said another person in the room ; "let 'Cash' in."

The door was opened and Simon entered, half-blinded by the sudden burst of light which streamed from the chandeliers and lamps, and was reflected in every direction by the mirrors which almost walled the room.   In the centre of the room was a small but unique " bar," the counter of which, except a small space occupied by a sliding door at which customers were served, was enclosed with burnished brass rods. Within this " magic circle" stood a pock-marked clerk, who vended to the company wines and liquors too costly to be imbibed by any but men of fortune or gamesters, who, alternately rich and penniless, indulge every appetite without stint while they have the means ; eating viands and drinking wines one day, which a prince might not disdain, to fast entirely the next, or make a disgusting meal from the dirty counter of a miserable eating-house.   Disposed at regular intervals around the room, were tables for the various games usually played ; all of them thronged with eager " customers," and covered with heavy piles of doubloons, and dollars, and bank notes.   Of these tables the " tiger" claimed three—for faro was predominant in those days, when a cell in the penitentiary was not the penalty for exhibiting it.   Most of the persons in the room were well-dressed, and a large proportion members of the legislature.   There was very little noise, no loud swearing, but very deep playing.

As Simon entered, he made his rustic bow, and in an easy, familiar way, saluted the company with

"Good evenin' gentle*men!*"

No one seemed inclined to acknowledge, on behalf of the company, their pleasure at seeing Captain Suggs. Indeed, nobody appeared to notice him at all after the first half second. The Captain, therefore, repeated his salutation:

"*I say*, GOOD EVENIN', gentle*men!*"

Notwithstanding the emphasis with which the words were re-spoken, there was only a slight laugh from some of the company, and the Captain began to feel a little awkward standing up before so many strangers. While he was hesitating whether to begin business at once by walking up to one of the faro tables and commencing the "fight," he overheard a young man standing a few feet from him, say to another,

"Jim, isn't that your uncle, General Witherspoon, who has been expected here for several days with a large drove of hogs?"

"By Jupiter," said the person addressed, "I believe it is; though I'm not certain, as I haven't seen him since I was a little fellow. But what makes *you* think it's him: you never saw him?"

"No, but he suits the description given of your uncle, very well—white hair, red eyes, wide mouth, and so forth. Does your uncle gamble?"

"They say he does; but my mother, who is his sister, knows hardly any more about him than the rest of the world. We've only seen him once in fifteen years. I'll de d—d," he added, looking steadfastly at Simon, "if that isn't he! He's as rich as mud, and a jovial old cock of a bachelor, so I must claim kin with him."

Simon could, of course, have no reasonable objection to being believed to be General Thomas Witherspoon, the rich hog drover from Kentucky. Not he! The idea pleased him excessively, and he determined if he was not respected as General Witherspoon for the remainder of that evening, it should be " somebody else's fault," not his! In a few minutes, indeed, it was whispered through the company, that the red-eyed man with white hair, was the wealthy field-officer who drove swine to increase his fortune ; and in consequence of this, Simon thought he discovered a very considerable improvement in the way of politeness, on the part of all present. The bare suspicion that he was rich, was sufficient to induce deference and attention.

Sauntering up to a faro bank with the intention of betting, while his money should hold out, with the spirit and liberality which General Witherspoon would have displayed had be been personally present, he called for

" Twenty, five-dollar checks, and that pretty toloble d—d quick!"

The dealer handed him the red checks, and he piled them upon the " ten."

" Grind on !" said Simon.

A card or two was dealt, and the keeper, with a profound bow, handed Simon twenty more red checks.

"Deal away," said Simon, heaping the additional checks on the same card.

Again the cards flew from the little box, and again Simon won.

Several persons were now over-looking the game, and among the rest, the young man who was so happy as to be the nephew of General Witherspoon.

"The old codger has nerve; I'll be d—d if he hasn't," said one.

"And money too," said another, "from the way he bets."

"To be sure he has," said a third; "that's the rich hog drover from Kentucky."

By this time Simon had won seven hundred dollars. But the Captain was not at all disposed to discontinue. "Now!" he thought was the "golden moment" in which to press his luck; "now!" the hour of the "tiger's" doom, when he should be completely flayed.

"That brings the fat in great fleeks as big as my arm!" observed the Captain, as he won the fifth consecutive bet: "it's hooray, brother John, every fire a turkey! as the boy said. Here goes again!" and he staked his winnings and the original stake on the Jack.

"Gracious heavens! General, I wouldn't stake so much on a single card," said a young man who was inclined to boot-lick any body suspected of having money.

"*You* wouldn't, young man," said the Captain, turning round and facing him, "bekase *you* never tote a pile of that size."

The obtrusive individual shrunk back under this rebuke, and the crowd voted Simon not only a man of spunk, but a man of wit.

At this moment the Jack won, and the Captain was better off, by fifteen hundred dollars, than when he entered the saloon.

"That's better—jist the least grain in the world better—than drivin' hogs from Kaintucky and sellin' 'em at four cents a pound!" triumphantly remarked Suggs.

The nephew of General Witherspoon was now confident that Captain Suggs was his uncle. He accordingly pushed up to him with—

"Don't you know me, uncle?" at the same time extending his hand.

Captain Suggs drew himself up with as much dignity as he supposed the individual whom he personated would have assumed, and remarked that he did *not* know the young man then in his immediate presence.

"Don't know me, uncle. Why, I'm James Peyton, your sister's son. She has been expecting you for several days;" said the much-humbled nephew of the hog drover.

"All very well, Mr. Jeemes Peyton, but as this little world of ourn is tolloble d—d full of rascally impostors; and gentle*men* of my—that is to say—you see—persons that have got somethin', is apt to be tuk in, it stands a man in hand to be a leetle perticler. So jist answer me a strait forrard question or two," said the Captain, subjecting Mr. Peyton to a test, which if applied to himself, would have blown

him sky-high. But Simon was determined to place
his own identity as General Witherspoon above suspicion, by seeming to suspect something wrong about
Mr. James Peyton.

"Oh," said several of the crowd, "every body
knows he's the widow Peyton's son, and your nephew,
of course."

"Wait for the wagin, gentle*men*," said Simon;
"*every body* has give me several sons, which, as I
aint married, I don't want, and" added he with a
very facetious wink and smile, "I don't care about
takin' a nephy on the same terms without he's giniwine."

"Oh, he's genuine," said several at once.

"Hold on, gentle*men ;* this young man might want
to borrow money of me—"

Mr. Peyton protested against any such supposition.

"Oh, well!" said the Captain, "*I* might want to
borrow of *you*, and—"

Mr. Peyton signified his willingness to lend his
uncle the last dollar in his pocket book.

"Very good! very good! but *I* happen to be a little
notiony about sich matters. It aint every man I'd
borrer from. Before I handle a man's money in the
way of borrerin, in the fust place I must know him to
be a gentleman ; in the second place, he must be my
friend ; and in the third place, I must think he's both
able and willin' to afford the accommodation"—and
the Captain paused and looked around to receive the
applause which he knew must be elicited by the
magnanimity of the sentiment.

The applause *did* come; and the crowd thought

while they gave it, how difficult and desirable a thing it would be, to lend money to General Thomas Witherspoon, the rich hog drover.

The Captain now resumed his examination of Mr. Peyton.

"What's your mother's fust name?" he asked.

"Sarah," said Mr. Peyton meekly.

"Right! so fur," said the Captain, with a smile of approval: "how many children has she?"

"Two: myself and brother Tom."

"Right again!" observed the Captain. "Tom, gentle*men*," added he, turning to the crowd, and venturing a shrewd guess; "Tom, gentle*men*, was named arter *me*. Warn't he, sir?" said he to Mr. Peyton, sternly.

"He was, sir—his name is Thomas Witherspoon."

Captain Suggs bobbed his head at the company, as much as to say, "*I* knew it;" and the crowd in their own minds, decided that the *ci-devant* General Witherspoon was "a devilish sharp old cock"—and the crowd wasn't far out of the way.

Simon was not acting in this matter without an object. He intended to make a bold attempt to win a small fortune, and he thought it quite possible he should lose the money he had won; in which case it would be convenient to have the credit of General Witherspoon to operate upon.

"Gentle*men*," said he to the company, with whom he had become vastly popular; "your attention, *one* moment, ef you please!"

The company accorded him its most obsequious attention.

F

" Come here, Jeemes!"

Mr. James Peyton approached to within eighteen inches of his supposititious uncle, who raised his hands above the young man's head, in the most impressive manner.

" One and all, gentle*men*," said he, " I call on you to witness that I reckognize this here young man as my proper, giniwine nephy—my sister Sally's son; and wish him respected as sich. Jeemes, hug your old uncle!"

Young Mr. James Peyton and Captain Simon Suggs then embraced. Several of the bystanders laughed, but a large majority sympathized with the Captain. A few wept at the affecting sight, and one person expressed the opinion that nothing so soul-moving had ever before taken place in the city of Tuskaloosa. As for Simon, the tears rolled down his face, as naturally as if they had been called forth by real emotion, instead of being pumped up mechanically to give effect to the scene.

Captain Suggs now renewed the engagement with the tiger, which had been temporarily suspended that he might satisfy himself of the identity of James Peyton. But the " fickle goddess," jealous of his attention to the nephew of General Witherspoon, had deserted him in a pet.

" Thar goes a dozen d—d fine, fat hogs!" said the Captain, as the bank won a bet of two hundred dollars.

Suggs shifted about from card to card, but the bank won always! At last he thought it best to return to the " ten," upon which he bet five hundred dollars.

"Now, I'll wool you," said he.

"Next time!" said the dealer, as he threw the winning card upon his own pile.

"That makes my hogs squeal," said the Captain; and every body admired the fine wit and nerve of the hog drover.

In half an hour Suggs was " as flat as a flounder." Not a dollar remained of his winnings or his original stake. It was, therefore, time to " run his face," or rather, the " face" of General Witherspoon.

" Could a body bet a few mighty fine bacon hogs, agin money at this table?" he inquired.

The dealer would be happy to accommodate the General, upon his word of honor.

It was not long before Suggs had bet off a very considerable number of the very fine hogs in General Witherspoon's uncommonly fine drove. He began to feel, too, as if a meeting with the veritable drover might be very disagreeable. He began, therefore, to entertain serious notions of borrowing some money and leaving in the stage, that night, for Greensboro'. Honor demanded, however, that he should " settle" to the satisfaction of the dealer. He accordingly called

" Jeemes!"

Mr. Peyton responded very promptly to the call.

"Now," said Simon, "Jeemes, I'm a little behind to this gentleman here, and I'm obleeged to go to Greensboro' in to-night's stage, on account of seein' ef I can engage pork thar. Now ef *I* shouldn't be *here*, when my hogs *come in*, do *you*, Jeemes, take this gentleman to wharever the boys puts 'em up, and let him pick thirty of the finest in the drove. D'ye *hear*, Jeemes?"

James promised to attend to the delivery of the hogs.

"Is that satisfactory?" asked Simon.

"Perfectly," said the dealer; "let's take a drink."

Before the Captain went up to the bar to drink, he patted "Jeemes" upon the shoulder, and intimated that he desired to speak to him privately. Mr. Peyton was highly delighted at this mark of his rich uncle's confidence, and turned his head to see whether the company noted it. Having ascertained that they did, he accompanied his uncle to an unoccupied part of the saloon.

"Jeemes," said the Captain thoughtfully, "has your—mother bought—her—her—pork yet?"

James said she had not.

"Well, Jeemes, when my drove comes in, do you go down and pick her out ten of the best. Tell the boys to show you them new breed—the Berkshears."

Mr. Peyton made his grateful acknowledgements for his uncle's generosity, and they started back towards the crowd. Before they had advanced more than a couple of steps, however—

"Stop!" said Simon, "I'd like to a' forgot. Have you as much as a couple of hunderd by you, Jeemes, that I could use twell I git back from Greensboro'?"

Mr. Peyton was very sorry he hadn't more than fifty dollars about him. His uncle could take that, however—as he did forthwith—and he would "jump about" and get the balance in ten minutes.

"Don't do it, ef it's ary trouble at all, Jeemes," said the Captain cunningly.

But Mr. James Peyton was determined that he would "raise the wind" for his uncle, let the "trouble" be what it might; and so energetic were his endeavours, that in a few moments he returned to the Captain and handed him the desired amount.

"Much obleeged to you, Jeemes; I'll remember you for this;" and no doubt the Captain has kept his word; for whenever he makes a promise which it costs nothing to perform, Captain Simon Suggs is the most punctual of men.

After Suggs had taken a glass of "sperrets" with his friend the dealer—whom he assured he considered the "smartest and cleverest" fellow out of Kentucky —he wished to retire. But just as he was leaving, it was suggested in his hearing, that an oyster supper would be no inappropriate way of testifying his joy at meeting his clever nephew and so many true-hearted friends.

"Ah, gentlemen, the old hog drover's broke now, or he'd be proud to treat to something of the sort. They've knocked the leaf fat outen him to-night, in wads as big as mattock handles," observed Suggs, looking at the bar-keeper out of the corner of his left eye.

"Any thing this house affords is at the disposal of General Witherspoon," said the bar-keeeper.

"Well! well!" said Simon, "you're all so clever,

I must stand it I suppose, tho' I oughtn't to be so extravagant."

"Take the crowd, sir?"

"Certainly," said Simon.

"How much champagne, General?"

"I reckon we can make out with a couple of baskets," said the Captain, who was determined to sustain any reputation for liberality which General Witherspoon might, perchance, possess.

There was a considerable ringing of bells for a brief space, and then a door which Simon hadn't before seen, was thrown open, and the company ushered into a handsome supping apartment. Seated at the convivial boa..l, the Captain outshone himself; and to this day, some of the *bon mots* which escape' him on that occasion, are remembered and repeated.

At length, after the proper quantity of champagne and oysters had been swallowed, the young man whom Simon had so signally rebuked early in the evening, rose and remarked that he had a sentiment to propose: "I give you, gentlemen," said he, "the health of General Witherspoon. Long may he live, and often may he visit our city and partake of its hospitalities!"

Thunders of applause followed this toast, and Suggs, as in duty bound, got up in his chair to respond.

"Gentlemen," said he "I'm devilish glad to see you all, and much obleeged to you, besides. You are the finest people I ever was amongst, and treat me a d—d sight better than they do at home"— which was a fact! "Hows'ever, I'm a poor hand to speak, but here's wishing of luck to you all"—and then wickedly seeming to blunder in his little speech —"and if I forgit you, I'll be d—d if you'll ever forgit me!"

Again there was a mixed noise of human voices, plates, knives and forks, glasses and wine bottles, and then the company agreed to disperse. "What a noble-hearted fellow!" exclaimed a dozen in a breath, as they were leaving.

As Simon and Peyton passed out, the bar-keeper handed the former a slip of paper, containing such items as—"twenty-seven dozen of oysters, twenty-seven dollars; two baskets of champagne, thirty-six dollars,"—making a grand total of sixty-three dollars.

The Captain, who "felt his wine," only hiccoughed, nodded at Peyton, and observed.

"Jeemes, you'll attend to this?"

"Jeemes" said he would, and the pair walked out and bent their way to the stage-office, where the Greensboro' coach was already drawn up. Simon wouldn't wake the hotel keeper to get his saddlebags, because, as he said, he would probably return in a day or two.

"Jeemes," said he, as he held that individual's hand; "Jeemes, has your mother bought her pork yet?"

"No, sir," said Peyton, "you know you told me to take ten of your hogs for her—don't you recollect?"

"Don't do that," said Simon, sternly.

Peyton stood aghast! "Why sir?" he asked.

" Take TWENTY !" said the Captain, and wringing
the hand he held, he bounced into the coach, which
whirled away, leaving Mr. James Peyton on the
pavement, in profound contemplation of the boundless generosity of his uncle, General Thomas Witherspoon of Kentucky!

CHAPTER THE SIXTH.

SIMON SPECULATES AGAIN.

THERE are few of the old settlers of the Creek territory in Alabama, who do not recollect the great Indian Council held at Dudley's store, in Tallapoosa county, in September of the year 1835. In those days, an occasion of the sort drew together white man and Indian from all quarters of the " nation"—the one to cheat, the other to be cheated. The agent appointed by the Government to " certify" the sales of Indian lands was always in attendance; so that the scene was generally one of active traffic. The industrious speculator, with his assistant, the wily interpreter, kept unceasingly at work in the business of fraud; and by every species and art of persuasion, sought—and, sooner or later, succeeded—in drawing the untutored children of the forest into their nets. If foiled once, twice, thrice, a dozen times, still they kept up the pursuit. It was ever the constant trailing of the slow-track dog, from whose fangs there was no final escape!

And where are these speculators NOW?—those lords of the soil!—the men of dollars—the fortune-makers who bought with hundreds what was worth thousands!—they to whom every revolution of the sun brought a reduplication of their wealth! Where are they, and what are they, now! They have been smitten by the hand of retributive justice! The curse of their victims has fastened upon them, and nine out of ten are houseless, outcast, bankrupt! In the flitting of ten years, the larger portion have lost money, lands, character, every thing! And the few who still retain somewhat of their once lordly possessions, mark its steady, unaccountable diminution, and strive vainly to avert their irresistible fate—an old age of shame and beggary. They are cursed, all of them—blighted, root and trunk and limb! The Creek is avenged! Avenged, and for *what!* ask you, reader? Let us tell you a little story!

We knew, at the period to which this chapter refers, an Indian who refused to sell his land on any terms. He was a sturdy, independent fellow; one of the few who would not be contaminated by intercourse with the whites. His land was very valuable, and many speculators were, therefore, anxious to purchase it. So desirable was it, that several would, perhaps, have paid the "Sky chief" half its actual value to obtain it; but the "Sky chief" resolutely persisted in resisting all their arts; and he was too well known to make it practicable to get it, by hiring some thieving Indian to personate him before the certifying agent. But "Sudo Micco" had a daughter, a very pretty girl of fifteen—slightly made, with a Grecian face, and long coal-black hair; and her name was Litka. Well! Litka went to a dance—the green corn dance of her people—and it was conceded, that in her new calico frock and profusion of blue and red ribbons, and her silver buckles, she was the handsomest girl on the ground. Among her admirers was a young man named Eggleston—a sub-partner, or "striker," of the great Columbus Land Company. Eggleston told a sweet tale to the Indian girl, and she—as he was a very handsome young man—believed it all. He told her that he would marry her and take care of her, and of her father; and that when the rest of the tribe should be forced to Arkansas, *they* could stay with him in their old home, by the graves of their fathers. The "long and short" of all this was, that the white man and Indian girl were married according to the Creek custom; Sudo Micco having willingly assented to an arrangement by which he expected to be permitted to remain upon the soil which contained the bones of his ancestors. For a few months Eggleston treated Litka and Sudo Micco very well, and they confided in him implicitly. Then he told his wife that her father must "certify" his land to him, or "bad white men" might contrive to get it. Litka told the old "Sky chief" what her husband said, and the simple-minded Indian said it was "a good talk," and that his "white man son" should do as he pleased. So the "Sky chief" "certified" his land to his son-in-law; and the certifying agent saw a thousand silver dollars paid to the Indian, who within ten minutes afterwards returned them. Then Eggleston deserted Litka, and sold the land for three thousand dollars. Sudo Micco fumed and raved—but what good could that do? And Litka, poor thing! was almost broken-hearted. And last of all, Sudo Micco begged his son-in-law, as he had got his land for nothing, and his daughter was too near her confinement to travel on foot, to get him a little wagon and a horse to take them to Arkansas.

But Eggleston laughed in his face, and told him that a wagon would cost too much money. So Sudo Micco was compelled to wait until the Government removed his people; and then he went in one of the "public" wagons, among the "*poor*" of his tribe. FOR THIS, AND SUCH AS THIS—as we have shown—IS THE CREEK AVENGED!

But we set out to tell about the council at Dudley's, and here we are writing episodes about Creek frauds, as long almost, as the catalogue of Creek wrongs! We will come back to the starting point. It was a right beautiful sight to look at—the camp-fires of five thousand Indians, that burned at every point of the circular ridge which enclosed Dudley's trading establishment; and it was thrilling to hear the wild whoopings, and wilder songs of the "natives," as they danced and capered about their respective encampments—on the first night of the council. It was a little alarming too, to witness the occasional miniature battle between "towns" which, like the Highland clans, had their feuds of immemorial date.

"Coop! coop! hee!" shouts a champion of the Cohomutka-Gartska town, the principal family of which was that which rejoiced in the name of "Deer." "The Oakfuskee people are all cowards —they run like rabbits! They are liars! They have two tongues! Coop! coop! hee-e-e! the Alligator family is mixed-blooded! they come from the runaway Seminole and the runlet-making Cherokee! The "Deer" people can beat the Alligator people till they beg for their hides!" Then the representative of the chivalrous "Deer" people struts before his

camp-fire, gesticulating violently, and expressing his
contempt of his Alligator brethren, by all sorts of
grotesque attitudes; while the women and children
about the fire, declare that Cho-yoholo, (the Screaming Deer,) is a great warrior, and can flog every Alligator of them all by himself.

Presently, a representative of the Oakfuskee town,
and the Alligator family, strides out in front of his
temporary lodge, which is about a hundred yards
from the encampment of his hostile neighbours.

"Eep! eep! e-e-e-yah!" he shouts, so shrilly that
your "skin creeps." "The dog of Cohomutka-
Gartska brags like a child, but his heart is the heart
of the poor little toad, that tries to hop away at dusk
from the black-snake! The Alligators are brave;
their hearts are big and full of red blood. If the
thieving Deer people will send one of their best war-
riors half-way, the Alligator people will send an old
woman to meet him! Eep! eep! e-e-e-yah!" And
then Hulputta Hardjo (Mad Alligator,) slaps his
hands upon his hips, and turns contemptuously away.

In a few moments the "Alligators" and "Deer,"
and all their friends, are engaged pell mell, in a fight
with clubs, rocks, knives, teeth, hands and toes;
while the Indians in their neighbourhood, who have
no particular interest in the affray, hold torches to
enable the combatants on both sides, to deal their
blows more effectively.

As a matter of course, our friend and hero the Captain, was at the council. He was never known to
absent himself from any such congregation. If out
of funds, he went to "recruit;" if he had a "stake,"

he attended that the "Tiger"—which then was peripatetic and almost omnipresent, because at that time our supreme court judges had not muzzled him —might have an opportunity of devouring it. On the present occasion he really had business; for he had brought with him to be "certified"—that is, to submit for the approval of the government agent, a contract for the sale of her land—an Indian woman, whose "reserve" was an excellent one. Simon had contracted to pay her two hundred dollars and three blankets for it; and as she happened to take a liking to him, she preferred that he should have it at that price, to selling to others who were offering her a thousand. In this, the "Big Widow" but illustrated a waywardness, amounting to absolute stupidity, which was common among the Creeks. It was in vain that she was assailed on all hands, and persuaded to accept a larger price. "The Mad Bird,"—so was the Captain called by the Indians—she would observe, "would give her three blankets and two hundred dollars, and she would give him her land. The Mad Bird was a good friend, and had a sweet tongue; and if she gave her land to any body else, he would have the "big mad," and then he wouldn't give her tobacco and *sweet water* any more.

There was but one obstacle in the way of the Captain's making a very handsome speculation; but that was a very serious one under present circumstances: he did't happen to have the money. True, we have said in another chapter, that the Captain disdained to embark in speculations requiring the investment of cash capital; but the reader must do us the justice to recollect, that "there is no rule without an exception." *In a general way*, we know we have asserted, and we here reassert, that Simon Suggs could, by the force of his own genius, speculate without funds; but we would like to know how any reasonable man could expect Captain Suggs, or any one else, to purchase an Indian's land without money, when by an act of Congress it was requisite that the appraised price should be paid *in the presence of the agent.* Could the Captain but have had the use, for only ten minutes, of two hundred dollars, he could easily have owned the Big Widow's " low grounds," and paid the money back, too, had he chosen so to do Unfortunately, however, such a loan was not to be obtained, and his efforts to " make the raise," caused it to be known that he had no means of paying the widow for her land at that time. This fact—for it was so regarded, very correctly—gave each of a half-dozen other speculators on the ground, encouragement to hope that *he* might be the lucky purchaser. They then beset the old woman, one after another, so that she had scarcely time to cook the sophky for her children, or drink a spoonful herself. Still she resolutely adhered to her promise to the Mad Bird, and would *not* sell to any other. At length the Captain hit upon an expedient, and calling together his rivals at the widow's camp, he harangued them:

" Gentle*men*," said he, " you all know this here old widder Injun is under promise to me, to sell me her land ! Now I takes it to be d—d ongentlemanly, gentle*men*, that you all, bein' in the same line o' business with myself, should endeavour to take advantage of a feller's bein' a leetle low down, and steal his *honest* contract. But, hows'ever, gentle*men*, that's not the pint of my discourse, which are shortly this: ef any of you, gentle*men*, will shell out the necessary trimmins, so's that the old lady, here, can pass muster before the agent, I'll let him have an even intrust with me in the land! Which of you'll do it, gentle*men*?—don't all speak at oncet!"

Colonel Bryan whispered to General Lawson, and Major Taylor whispered to Mr. Goodwin; and then they all whispered together, and then they all stopped and looked at one another, as not knowing what to say.

"Out with it, gentle*men*," exclaimed Simon, "don't spile the shape on it, by keepin' it in!"

"Can't stand it, Simon," said Lawson.

"As good as wheat!" replied Simon; but I'll eat Satan raw and onsalted, ef any of you ever git a foot of that land. I'm not quite as fur down as you think. There's an old friend of mine not twenty mile from here, that's got three or four hamper baskets-full o' Mexicans, and I guess I can git a bushel or so, jist to ease the pain, twell a feller can git the chance to have the tooth drawd!" Then turning to the Big Widow, and indicating with his finger the point in he heavens at which the sun would be the next morning at ten o'clock, he told her, if he was not back by the time it got there, she might believe that he had failed to procure the money, and sell to whom she pleased. He then mounted his pony and galloped off.

The next day, at a very early hour, the specula-

" Mr Suggs, ' said he, ' I'd like to have an interest in your contract, and I m
willing to pay for it   I'll find the money to pay the Indian

tors were tugging at the Big Widow, each striving to induce her to sell to himself in case Simon should not return, upon which they all confidently calculated. Each made so tempting an offer, that the poor woman knew not which to accept; or rather, she accepted them all in turn. The land was worth fifteen hundred dollars, and eight hundred were already bid when Simon's limit was within a half hour of its expiration. At length the sun reached the ten o'clock point, and the Captain not appearing, the rivals, among them, pushed and pulled the old squaw up to the shed under which the agent was "certifying." Here a general fight ensued; Colonel Bryan striking Major Taylor across the nose in the enthusiasm of the moment; and General Lawson doing something of the same sort for Mr. Goodwin, because he apprehended that the row would become general, and that those would fare best, who struck soonest and hardest.

Just at this moment Simon dashed up at full speed.

"Don't break *all* the crockery, gentle*men*," he shouted. "Jist give a poor man a chance to make an honest contract, won't ye!"

"The Mad Bird has come back, I will give my land to him," said the Big Widow, approaching Simon, who had dismounted, and was bending beneath the weight of a very plethoric pair of saddle-bags.

The fighting ceased when Suggs made his appearance, and there was a moment's silence. The first to break it was General Lawson. "Mr. Suggs," said he, "I'd like to have an interest in your contract, and I'm willing to pay for it. I'll find the money to pay the Indian, and give you an interest of one- hird."

"Not 'thout I was willing—would ye?" asked Suggs jeeringly.

"I'll do better than that," said Taylor, wiping the blood from his nose; "I'll furnish the money and give you half the land sells for when we part with it!'"

"Very proverbly," remarked Simon, "very proverbly! But onless some on ye counts me out five hundred, and furnishes your own money to buy the land, I shall have to onlock these here," patting his saddle-bags, "and buy it for myself."

"I'll do it!" said Colonel Bryan, who had been making a calculation on the inside of the crown of his hat—"I'll do it!"

"Ah!" said Suggs, "*that's* what made the chicken's squall! *You're* the man I'm a-huntin'! Draw your weepins!"

The land was forthwith "certified" to Suggs, who immediately transferred it to Bryan.

"Now, gentle*men*," said the Captain, every body's satisfied—aint they?"

"If they *aint*, they *ought* to be," replied Colonel Bryan, who was delighted with his bargain.

"I think so too," remarked Suggs, "and bein' as that's the case," he continued, opening his saddle-bags, "I'll throw out these here *rocks and old iron*, for its *mighty* tiresome to a horse!" and the Captain *did* throw out the rocks and old iron!

The speculators vanished!

"This here's a mighty hard world," murmured the

Captain to himself, musingly, " to git along in. Ef a feller don't make every aidge cut, he's in the background directly. It's tile and strive, and tussle every way, to make an honest livin'. Well!" he continued, in a strain of unusual piety, as he threw up and caught again, a rouleau of dollars; " Well! thar *is* a Providence that purvides; and ef a man will *only* stand squar' up to what's right, it *will* prosper his endeavours to make somethin' to feed his children on! Yes, thar *is* a Providence! I should like to see the man would say thar aint. I don't hold with no sich. Ef a man says thar aint no Providence, you may be sure thar's something wrong *here*;" striking in the region of his vest pocket—" and *that* man will swindle you, ef he can—CERTIN!"

CHAPTER THE SEVENTH.

SIMON BECOMES CAPTAIN.

By reference to memoranda, contemporaneously taken, of incidents to be recorded in the memoirs of Captain Suggs, we find that we have reached the most important period in the history of our hero—his assumption of a military command. And we beg the reader to believe, that we approach this portion of our subject with a profound regret at our own incapacity for its proper illumination. Would that thy pen, O! Kendall, were ours! Then would thy hero and ours —the nation's Jackson and the country's Suggs—go down to far posterity, equal in fame and honors, as in deeds! But so the immortal gods have not decreed! Not to Suggs was Amos given! Aye, jealous of his mighty feats, the thundering Jove denied an historian worthy of his puissance! Would that, like Cæsar, he could write himself! Then, indeed, should Harvard yield him honors, and his country—justice!

Early in May of the year of grace—and excessive bank issues—1836, the Creek war was discovered to have broken out. During that month several persons, residing in the county of Tallapoosa, were cruelly murdered by the "inhuman savages;" and an exceedingly large number of the peaceful citizens of the state—men, women and children—excessively frightened. Consternation seized all! "Shrieks inhuman" rent the air! The more remote from the scenes of blood, the greater the noise. The yeomanry of the country—those to whom, as we are annually told, the nation looks with confidence in all her perils—packed up their carts and wagons, and "incontinently" departed for more peaceful regions! We think we see them now, "strung along the road," a day or two after the intelligence of the massacres below had reached the "settlement" of Captain Suggs! There goes old man Simmons, with his wife and three daughters, together with two feather beds, a few chairs, and a small assortment of pots and ovens, in a cart drawn by a bob-tail, gray pony. On the topmost bed, and forming the apex of this pile of animate and inanimate "luggage," sits the old tom-cat, whom the youngest daughter would not suffer to remain lest he might come to harm. "Who knows," she exclaims, "*what* they might do to the poor old fellow?" On they toil! the old man's head, ever and anon, turned back to see if they are pursued by the remorseless foe; while the wife and daughters scream direfully, every ten minutes, as they discover in the distance a cow or a hog—"Oh, they'll kill us! they'll skelp us! they'll tar us all *to* pieces! Oh, Lord! daddy! oh, Lord!" But the old tom-cat sits there, gravely and quietly, the very incarnation of tom philosophy!

It was on Sunday that the alarm was sounded in the "Suggs settlement," and most of the neighbours were in attendance upon the "preaching of the word" by brother Snufflenosey, at Poplar Spring meeting-house, when the "runner" who brought the woful tidings, disclosed them at old Tom Rollins', by

yelling, as he sat on his horse before the door,—"the
Injuns is a-killin every body below! I aint got time
to stop! tell the neighbours!"   Now, old Mr. Rollins
and the "gals" were already at meeting, but the old
lady, having staid behind "to fix up a leetle," was,
at the identical moment of the messenger's arrival, *en
chemise* before a very small glass set in a frame of red
paper, preparing to adorn her person with divers new
articles of apparel, inclusive of a new blue-and-red-
calico gown.   But no sooner did her mind comprehend the purport of the words from without, than she
sprang out of the house, "accoutred as she was,"
shrieking at every bound, "the Injuns! the Injuns!"—nor stopped until with face, neck, and bosom
crimson as a strutting gobbler's snout, she burst into
the meeting-house, and having once more screamed
"the Injuns!" fell exhausted, at full length, upon the
floor. "Will any of the breethring lend me a horse?"
asked the Reverend Mr. Snufflenosey, wildly, as he
bounded out of the pulpit, in very creditable style—
"Wont *none* of you lend me one?" he repeated emphatically; and obtaining no answer, dashed off pre-
cipitately afoot! Then went up to Heaven the screams
of fifty frightened women, in one vast discord, more
dreadful than the war-squalls of an hundred cats in
fiercest battle. Men, too, looked pale and trembled;
while, strange to relate, all of the dozen young babies
in attendance silently dilated their astonished eyes—
struck utterly dumb at being so signally beaten at
their own peculiar game!

At length an understanding was somehow effected,
that Taylor's store, five miles thence, should be the

place of rendezvous, for that night at least; and then Mr. Snufflenosey's congregation tumbled itself forth as expeditiously as was possible.

"Simon was "duly" at the store with his family, when the wagon, cart, and pony loads of "badly-scared" mortality began to arrive in the afternoon. He was there of course, and he was in his element. Not that Suggs is particularly fond of danger—albeit, he is a hero—but because he delighted in the noise and confusion, the fun and the free drinking, incident to such occasions. And he enjoyed these to the uttermost now, because he was well informed as to the state of feeling of the Indians, in all the country for ten miles around, and knew there was no danger. But Simon did not disclose this to the terrified throng at the store. Not he! Suggs was never the man to destroy his own importance in that sort of way. On the contrary, he magnified the danger, and endeavoured to impress upon the minds of the miscellaneous crowd "then and there" assembled, that he, Simon Suggs, was the only man at whose hands they could expect a deliverance from the imminent peril which impended.

"Gentle*men*," said he impressively, "this here is a critercle time; the wild savage of the forest are beginnin' of a bloody, hostile war, which they're not a-goin' to spar nither age nor sek—not even to the women and children!"

"Gracious Lord above! what *is* a body to do!" exclaimed the portly widow Haycock, who was accounted wealthy, in consideration of the fact that she had a hundred dollars in money, and was the undisputed owner of one entire negro—" we shall all be skelped, and our truck all burnt up and destr'yed! What shall we do!"

" That's the question," remarked Simon, as he stooped to draw a glass of whiskey from a barrel of that article—the only thing on sale in the " store"— " that's the question. Now, as for you women-folks"—here Suggs dropped a lump of brown sugar in his whiskey, and began to stir it with his finger, looking intently in the tumbler, the while—" as for you women-folks, it's plain enough what *you*'ve got to do"—here Simon tasted the liquor and added a little more sugar—" plain *enough!* You've only got to look to the Lord and hold your jaws; for that's all you *kin* do! But what's the 'sponsible *men*"—tak-ing his finger out of the tumbler, and drawing it through his mouth—" of this crowd to do? The inemy will be down upon us right away, and before mornin' "—Simon drank half the whiskey—" blood will flow like—like"—the Captain was bothered for a simile, and looked around the room for one, but finding none, continued—" like all the world! Yes, like all the world"—an idea suggested itself—" and the Tallapussey river! It'll pour out," he continued, as his fancy got rightly to work, " like a great guljin ocean!—d—d ef it don't!" And then Simon swal-lowed the rest of the whiskey, threw the tumbler down, and looked around to observe the effect of this brilliant exordium.

The effect was tremendous!

Mrs. Haycock clasped her hands convulsively, and rolled up her eyes until the " whites" only could be seen. Old Mrs. Rollins—who by this time was fully clothed—and her two daughters had what Simon termed the "high-strikes" in one corner of the room, and kicked up their heels at a prodigious rate; while in another, a group of young women hugged one another most affectionately, sobbing hysterically all the time. ¯Old granny Gilbreth sat in the middle of the floor, rocking her body back and forth, striking the palms of her hands on the planks as she bent forward, and clapping them together as she re-attained the perpendicular.

"My apinion," continued Simon, as he stooped to draw another tumbler of whiskey; "my apinion, folks, is this here. We ought to form a company right away, and make some man capting that aint afeard to fight—mind what I say, now—*that-aint-afeard-to-fight!*—some sober, stiddy feller"—here he sipped a little from the tumbler—"that's a good hand to manage women and keep 'em from hollerin—which they're a-needin' somethin' of the sort most damdibly, and I eech to git holt o' that one a-making that devilish racket in the corner, thar"—the noise in the corner was suddenly suspended—"and more'n all, a man that's acquainted with the country and the ways of the Injuns!" Having thus spoken, Suggs drank off the rest of the whiskey, threw himself into a military attitude, and awaited a reply.

"Suggs is the man," shouted twenty voices.

"Keep close to *him*, and you'll never git hurt," said a diminutive, yellow-faced, spindle-legged young man.

"D'ye think so now?" exclaimed Simon furiously,

as he "planted" a tremendous kick on that part of
the joker's person at which the boot's point is most
naturally directed. "D'ye think so, now? Take
that along, and next time keep your jaw, you slink,
or I'll kick more clay outen you in a minute, than
you can eat again in a month, you durned, little, dirt-
eatin' deer-face!"

"Keep the children outen the way," said the little
fellow, as he lay sprawling in the farthest corner of
the room; "ef you don't, *Cap'en* Suggs will whip
'em all. He's a sight on children and people what's
got the *yaller janders!*"

Simon heeded not the sarcasm, but turning to the
men he asked—

"Now gentlemen, who'll you have for capting?"

"Suggs! Suggs! Suggs!" shouted a score and a
half of masculine voices.

The women said nothing—only frowned.

"Gentlemen," said Simon, a smile of gratified, but
subdued pride playing about his mouth; "Gentlemen, my respects—ladies, the same to you!"—and
the Captain bowed—"I'm more'n proud to sarve my
country at the head of sich an independent and pa-
triotic cumpany! Let who will run, gentlemen, Simon Suggs will allers be found sticking thar, like a
tick onder a cow's belly—"

"Whar do you aim to bury your dead Injuns,
Cap'en?" sarcastically inquired the little dirt-eater.

"I'll bury *you*, you little whifflin fice," said Captain Suggs in a rage; and he dashed at yellow-legs
furiously.

"Not afore a body's dead, I reckon," replied the

dirt-eater, running round the room, upsetting the
women and trampling the children, in his efforts
to escape. At last he gained the door, out of which
he bounced and ran off.

"Durn the little cuss," said the Captain, when he
saw that pursuit would be useless; "I oughtent to git
aggrawated at him, no how. He's a poor signifiken
runt, that's got the mark of the huckle-berry ponds
on his legs yit, whar the water come to when he was
a-getherin 'em, in his raisin' in Northkurliny. But I
must put a stop to sich, and that right away;" and
striding to the door, out of which he thrust his head,
he made proclamation: "Oh yes! gentle*men*! Oh yes!
This here store-house and two acres all round is now
onder *martial law!* If any man or woman don't mind
my orders, I'll have 'em shot right away; and children to be whipped accordin' to size. By order of
me, Simon Suggs, Capting of the"—the Captain
paused.

"Tallapoosy Vollantares," suggested Dick Can-
nifax.

"The Tallapoosy Vollantares," added Suggs,
adopting the suggestion; "so let every body look out,
and walk the chalk!"

Thus was formed the nucleus of that renowned
band of patriot soldiers, afterwards known as the
"FORTY THIEVES"—a name in the highest degree
inappropri te, inasmuch as the company, from the
very best evidence we have been able to procure,
never had upon its roll, at any time, a greater number of names than *thirty-nine!*

As became a prudent commander, Captain Suggs,

immediately after the proclamation of martial law, set
about rendering his position as strong as possible. A
rude rail fence near by was removed and made to en-
close the log store, and another building of the same
sort, which was used as a stable. · The company was
then paraded, and a big drink dealt out to each man,
and five men were detailed to serve as sentinels, one
at each corner of the enclosure, and one at the fence
in front of the store door.   The Captain then announced that he had appointed Andy Snipes, "fust
lewtenant," Bird Stinson " sekkunt ditto," and Dave
Lyon " sarjunt."

  The guard was set, the women summarily quieted,
the mass of the company stowed away in the stable
for the night; and the Captain and "Lewtenant
Snipes" sat down, with a bottle of bald-face between
them, to a social game of "six cards, seven up," by
a fire in the middle of the enclosure.   About this
time, the widow Haycock desired to possess herself
of a certain " plug" of tobacco, wherewithal to supply her pipe during the watches of the night.   The
tobacco was in her cart, which, with a dozen others,
stood in the road twenty steps or so from the front
door.   Now, as the widow Haycock was arrayed rather grotesquely—in a red-flannel wrapper, with a
cotton handkerchief about her head—she did not wish
to be seen as she passed out.   She therefore noise-
lessly slipped out, and, the sentinel having deserted
his post for a few moments to witness the playing between his officers, succeeded in reaching the cart un-
observed.   As she returned, however, with the weed
of comfort in her hand, she was challenged by the

"Stand!" said he, as the old lady was climbing the fence.

sentinel, who, hearing a slight noise, had come back to his post.

" Stand!" said he, as the old lady was climbing the fence.

"Blessed Master!" exclaimed Mrs. Haycock; but the soldier was too much frightened to observe that she spoke English, or to recognize her voice.

" Give the counter-sign or I'll shoot," said he, bringing his gun to a "present," but receding towards the fire as he spoke.

Instead of the counter-sign, Mrs. Haycock gave a scream, which the sentinel, in his fright, mistook for the war-whoop, and instantly fired. The widow dropped from the fence to the ground, on the outside, and the sentinel ran to the Captain's fire.

In a moment was heard the thundering voice of Captain Suggs:

" Turn out, men! Kumpny fo–r–m!"

The women in the store screamed, and the company formed immediately in front of the door. The Captain was convinced that the alarm was a humbug of some sort; but keeping up the farce, kept up his own importance.

"Bring your guns to a level with your breasts, and fire through the cracks of the fence!" he ordered.

An irregular volley was fired, which brought down a poney and a yoke of steers, haltered to their owner's carts in the road; and frightened "yellow-legs," (who had slyly taken lodgings in a little wagon,) nearly to death.

" Over the fence now! Hooraw! my galyunt vo-

luntares!" shouted the Captain, made enthusiastic by
the discharge of the guns.

The company scaled the fence.

"Now charge baggonets! Hooraw! Let 'em have
the cold steel, my brave boys!"

This manœuvre was executed admirably, considering the fact, that the company was entirely without
bayonets or a foe.   The men brought their pieces to
the proper position, ran ten steps, and finding nothing
else to pierce, drove the long, projecting ram-rods of
their rifles deep in the mellow earth!

"Pickle all them skelps, Cap'en Suggs, or they'll
spile!" said a derisive voice, which was recognized
as belonging to Yellow-legs, and a light form flitted
from among the wagons and carts, and was lost in the
darkness.

"Somebody kill that critter!" said Suggs, much
excited.   But the " critter" had " evaporated."

A careful examination of the field of battle was now
made, and the prostrate bodies of the pony, the oxen,
and the widow Haycock discovered, lying as they
had fallen.   From the last a slight moaning proceeded.   A light was soon brought.

"What's the matter, widder—hurt?" inquired
Suggs, raising up one of Mrs. Haycock's huge legs
upon his foot, by way of ascertaining how much life
was left.

"Only dead—that's all," said the widow as her
limb fell heavily upon the ground, with commendable
resignation.

"Pshaw!" said Suggs, " you aint bad hurt. Whar-
abouts did the bullet hit?"

"All over! *only* shot all to pieces' It makes *no* odds tho'—kleen through and through—I'm a-goin' mighty fast!" replied the widow, as four stout men raised her from the ground and carried her into the house, where her wounds were demonstrated to consist of a contusion on the bump of philo-progenitiveness, and the loss of a half square inch of the corrugated integument of her left knee.

Captain Suggs and Lieutenant Snipes now resumed their game.

"Lewtenant,"—said Suggs, as he dealt the cards—"we must—there's the tray for low—we must *court-martial* that old 'oman in the mornin'."

"'Twon't do, Capting—the tray I mean—to be sure we must! She's vierlated the rules of war!"

"And Yaller-legs, *too!*" said Suggs.

"Yes, yes; and Yaller-legs too, ef we kin ketch him," replied Lewtenant Snipes.

"Yes, d—d ef I don't!—court-martial 'em both, as sure as the sun rises—*drum-head* court-martial at that!"

CHAPTER THE EIGHTH.

CAPTAIN SUGGS AND LIEUTENANT SNIPES "COURT-MAR-
TIAL" MRS. HAYCOCK.

GREAT was the commotion at Fort Suggs on the
morning next after the occurrence of the events related in the last chapter. At FORT SUGGS we say—
for so had the Captain christened "Taylor's store"
and the enclosure thereof. Nor let any one repre-
hend him for so doing. It was but the exhibition of
a vanity, which, if not laudable, at least finds its sufficient excuse in a custom that has prevailed, "time
out of mind." Had not Romulus his Rome? Did
not the pugnacious son of Philip call his Egyptian
military settlement Alexandria? And—to descend
to later times and to cases more directly in point—is
there not a Fort Gaines in Georgia, and a Fort Jes-
sup in Florida? Who then shall carp, when we say
that Captain Simon Suggs bestowed *his* name upon
the spot strengthened by his wisdom, and protected
by his valour!

Great then, we repeat, was the commotion at FORT
SUGGS on the morning in question. The fact had become generally known—how could it be otherwise
with thirty women in the immediate vicinity'—that
Mrs. Haycock was to be "court-martialed" on that
morning; and the commotion was the consequence.
The widow herself was suffering great mental dis-
quietude on this subject, in addition to considerable

physical discomfort occasioned by the fall and rough handling of the previous night. Under such circumstances, it could hardly be expected that her woes would fail to find utterance. And it would have been equally unreasonable to suppose that her fellow gossips would restrain the natural propensity of the sex. Let the reader then, imagine—if he be not nervous—all the uproar and din which three dozen women can make under the most exciting circumstances, and he will have some faint conception of the commotion at Fort Suggs on the morning of the trial.

It was at an early hour; in fact—speaking according to the chronometrical standard in use at Fort Suggs—not more than " fust-drink time ;" when Captain Suggs took Lieutenant Snipes aside to consult with him in regard to some of the details of preparation for the court-martial.

" Snipes," said the Captain, as he seated himself a-straddle of the fence, and saw his lieutenant safely adjusted in a like position—" Snipes, as sure's you're born, thar's a diffikilty about this here court-martial. Now I want you to tell me *how* we're to hold a *drumhead* court-martial *when we aint got a drum!*"

Lieutenant Snipes looked very much puzzled, and in fact he *was* exceedingly puzzled, and he considered the matter for several moments, but could see no way by which the " diffikilty" might be surmounted. At length he remarked,

" It *does* look aukerd, Capting!"

" Yes. You see when these here court-martials is jumped up all of a sudden, like this, they're *ableeged* to be of the drum-head sort—that's what I've *allers* hearn. Well now, supposin' we was to hold one *without the drum*, and heng or shoot that everlastin' old she-devil; *would* the law jestify us in doin' so? Sometimes I sorter think it would, and then agin it looks sorter jubous. What's *your* apinion, Lewtenant?"

"That's it—what you jist said," replied Lieutenant Snipes, deferentially.

"Good!" said the Captain—"lewtenants ought allers to think jist as ther captings do. It's a good sign."

"It's what *I've* allers done, and what I allers *expects* to do," replied Snipes.

"Well, well!" remarked Suggs, whose chief object was to impress Snipes with the idea that the widow's life was in actual danger—and through his lieutenant, create that impression upon Mrs. Haycock herself, and all the rest—"Well, well, *don't* you believe that ef I was to git a bar'l, or somethin' else pretty nigh *like* a drum, and hold the court-martial by that—don't you believe *that* would justify us ef any thing was brought up hderarter, supposin' we was to condemn the old woman to deth?"

"Be'likes it would," said Snipes.

"I *know* it would!" said Suggs emphatically.

"*I* know so too!" remarked the lieutenant, with increased confidence.

"Well, now, all *that's* settled," said the Captain, with an air of satisfaction—"the next thing is, how are we agwine to put her to death?"

"Why, we aint *tried* her yit!" said Snipes.

"To be sure! to be sure! I'd forgot that!—but you know thar's no way to git round condemnin' of her—is thar?"

"No way as *I* see!"

"It's a painful duty, Lewtenant! a very painful duty, Lewtenant Snipes; and very distressin'. But the rules of war is very strict, you know!"

"*Very* strict," said Snipes.

"And officers must do ther duty, come what may."

"They're *ableeged* to," said the lieutenant.

"Ah! well!" remarked Captain Suggs with considerable emotion, "it'll be time enough to fix how we shall execute the old critter at the trial. You think the bar'l will do?"

"Jist as good as any thing," replied Snipes—"a bar'l and a drum's sorter alike, any way."

"Well, you'd better go and fix up as well as you kin, and the natur' of the case will admit. Officers oughter dress as well as they kin at sich times, ef no other. I must go and bresh up, myself." And with that, the consultation between Captain Suggs and Lieutenant Snipes, ended; the former going off to put himself a little more in military trim; while the latter industriously employed himself in disseminating the result of the conference.

It was with extreme difficulty that the Captain arranged his costume to his own satisfaction, and made it befitting so solemn and impressive an occasion. After a great deal of trouble however, he did contrive to cut a somewhat military figure. With a sword he was already "indifferently well" provided; having

found one—rusty and without a scabbard—some-
where about the premises. This he buckled, or
rather tied to his side with buckskin strings. He
wore at the time, the identical blue jeanes frock-coat
which has since become so familiar to the people of
Tallapoosa—it was then new, but on this there were,
of course, no epaulettes. Long time did Captain
Suggs employ himself in devising expedients to supply the deficiency. At length he hit it. His wife
had a large crimson pin-cushion, and this he fastened
upon his left shoulder, having first caused some white
cotton fringe to be attached to the outward edge. In
lieu of crimson sash, he fastened around his waist a
bright-red silk handkerchief, with only a few white
spots on it. And this was an admirable substitute,
except that it was almost too short to tie before, and
exhibited no inconsiderable portion of itself in a depending triangle behind. The chapeau now alone
remained to be managed. This was easily done.
Two sides of the brim of his capacious beaver were
stitched to the body of the hat, and at the fastening
on the left side, Mrs. Suggs sewed a cockade of red
ferreting, nearly as big as the bottom of a saucer.
Thus imposingly habited—and having first stuffed
the legs of his pantaloons into the tops of a very an-
tique pair of boots—Captain Simon Suggs went forth.

At the upper end of the enclosure, and standing
near an empty whiskey barrel, was Lieutenant Snipes.
He had not been so successful as the Captain in the
matter of his toilette. Around his black wool hat
was pasted, or stitched, a piece of deep purple gilt
paper, such as is often found upon bolts of linen.

Upon this was represented a battle between a lion and a unicorn ; and in a scroll above were certain letters, which as Lieutenant Snipes himself remarked, "did'nt spell nothing"—at least, nothing that he could comprehend. In his hand was the handle of a hoe, armed at one extremity with a rusty bayonet—the only weapon of its kind, at that moment, to be found in the whole garrison of Fort Suggs. Equipped thus, and provided with a dirty sheet of paper, a portable inkstand, (containing poke-berry juice,) and the stump of a pen—all of which were upon the head of the barrel—the doughty Lieutenant awaited the moment when it should please Captain Suggs to arraign the prisoner and proceed with the trial.

"Tallapoosy Vollantares, parade here!" thundered Captain Suggs, as he walked up to the barrel.

Very soon the "component parts" of the "Vollantares" were grouped about their Captain.

"Form in a straight line!" squealed Lieutenant Snipes.

The company took the form of a half-moon!

Captain Suggs now ordered Mrs. Haycock to be brought out; whereupon Snipes went into the back-room of the store, and directly appeared again, leading the widow—who limped considerably, and howled like a full pack of wolves—by the hand. The Captain, however, by a judicious threat of instant decapitation, reduced the noise to a series of mere sobbings.

"Hadn't we better fix some way to have some music," said Suggs, "and march round the house once, before we perceed with the trial?"

I

Lieutenant Snipes suggested that there was no drum or fife, as the Captain knew, on the premises; but that "uncle Billy Allen" was an excellent drummer, and Joe Nalls a first-rate performer on the fife, and that perhaps those individuals might, for the nonce, be induced to make vocal imitations of their respective instruments, and with their hands "go through the motions" indispensable to their proper effect. Captain Suggs immediately spoke to those gentlemen, and they "kindly consented" to serve, on the very equitable condition of receiving a "drink" each, as soon as the affair was over.

The "vollantares" were now formed in double files, and between the two columns Mrs. Haycock, supported by a female friend on each side, was placed.

"Music to the front!" shouted Suggs; and the order was promptly obeyed.

"Company! March!"

"Dub—dub—dub-a-dub-a-dub," went "uncle Billy Allen," inclining dangerously from the perpendicular, in order to support properly, a non-existent drum!

"Phee-ee-phee-fee," whistled Mr. Nalls, as his fingers played rapidly upon the holes of his imaginary fife!

And the company marched, as it was ordered. Suggs, of course, headed the array, walking backwards in order to inspect its movements; while Snipes, with his bayonet, walked alongside and kept a sharp eye on the prisoner. Thus they marched slowly around the enclosure, and returned to the spot whence they started.

"Halt! Form a round ring all round the drum!" ordered the Captain, pointing to the barrel.

The "vollantares" arranged themselves so as to describe, not exactly a mathematical circle, but a figure slightly approximating thereto, with the Captain, Lieutenant Snipes, and the widow, in the centre.

"Betsy Haycock," said Captain Suggs, "you're fotch up here accordin' to the rigelations of drumhead court-martial, for infringin' on the rules of war, by crossin' of the lines agin orders; and that too, when the fort was onder martial law. Ef you've got any thing to say agin havin' your life tuk, less hear it."

Poor Mrs. Haycock became livid; her eyes dilated, and all her features assumed that sudden sharpness which mortal terror often produces. Trembling in all her joints, and with pallid lips, she gasped,

"Mercy! mercy! Captain Suggs! For God's sake don't kill me—oh don't ef you please! I only went for my tobakker—for the love of the Lord *don't* murder me! Have mercy—I'll never—no never—as long—"

"It aint *me*," said the Captain interrupting her; "it aint *me* that's a-gwine to kill you; it's the *Rules of War*. The rules of war is mighty strict—aint they, Lewtenent Snipes?"

"*Powerful* strict!" said Snipes.

"You've 'fessed the crime," continued Suggs, "and ef me and the Lewtenant wanted to let you off ever so bad, the rules of war would lay us liable ef we was to. But come, Lewtenant Snipes," he added, addressing that person; "the prisoner has made her acknowledgements; take your pen and ink, and let's go and see what's to be done about it."

The Lieutenant took up his writing materials, and the couple retired to a corner of the fence, where they seated themselves upon the ground. Directly Snipes was seen to write; and then he picked up his pen and ink again, and they returned.

"What—what—what's it?" chokingly inquired the widow, as they re-assumed their positions at the barrel.

"Read out the judg*ment*," said Suggs with immense solemnity.

Snipes read what he had written in the fence-corner, as follows:

"**Whares, Betsy Haycock were brought up afore us, bein' charged with infringin' the rules of war by crossin' of the lines agin orders, and Fort Suggs bein' under martial law at the time, and likewise ecknowlidged she was gilty, Tharfore we have tried her eccordin to said rules of war, and condems her to be baggonetted to deth in one hour from this time, witness our hands and seals.**"

A paleness, more ghastly than that of death, come over the widow's face as she heard the sentence. Falling to the earth, she grovelled at the feet of Captain Suggs.

"Save me—pity—help! for God's sake! Oh don't kill me Captain Suggs!—beg for me, Mr. Snipes. Oh, you won't—I know you won't murder me' You're jest in fun!—aint you? You couldn't have

"A paleness more ghastly than that of death come over the widow's
face as she heard the sentence   Falling to the earth, she
groveled at the feet of Cap ain Suggs'

the *heart* to kill a poor woman creetur like me!"—
and then she added in a hoarse whisper—"I'll
humble myself to you, Captain Suggs! I'll git down
on my very knees, and kiss your shoe! Don't take
my life away with that—" she didn't finish the sentence, but shuddered all over, as she thought of
Snipes' rusty bayonet.

"Oh! Jimminny Crimminny! what a cussed old
fool!" exclaimed a voice from the fence-corner, outside, which was instantly recognized as belonging to
Yellow-legs—"he darsent no more kill you, 'an he
dar to fight an Injun!"

The widow looked up, but took no comfort from
the words. Captain Suggs, highly indignant, seized
a large stone and projected it with Titan-like force,
at the dirt-eater; but it struck the fence. Yellow-
legs, not at all alarmed, turned his back to Suggs,
and made a gesture expressive of the highest degree
of contempt, and then bounded off.

"Lewtenant, prepar' for execution!" said the Captain, as he returned to the barrel.

Mrs. Haycock renewed her lamentations and en-
treaties.

"I wish," said Suggs, in a fit of mental abstrac-
tion, but soliloquizing *aloud;* "thar *was* some way to
save her. But ef I was to let her off with a *fine*, I
might be layin' myself liable to be tried for my own
life."

"Oh yes! Captain Suggs, I'll pay any fine you'll
put on me—I'll give up all the money I've got, ef
you'll jest let me off—do now, dear Captain—"

"Hey? What? Have *I* been talkin' out loud?"

inquired Suggs, starting with a disconcerted look from his reverie.

"Yes, yes!" answered the widow with great earnestness; "you said ef I'd pay a fine, you'd spar my life—didn't you now, *dear, good* Captain Suggs?"

"Ef I did, I oughent to 'a done it. I don't think I'd be jestified ef I was to let you off. The rules of war would hold *me* 'countable ef I did—don't you think they would, Lewtenant?"

"*Mighty* apt!" said Snipes, as he sharpened the end of his rusty bayonet on a fragment of rock, by way of preparing for the execution of the widow.

Mrs. Haycock adjured Captain Suggs by his affection for his own offspring, to impose a fine, instead of "makin' her poor fatherless children, orfins!" Tears came into Suggs' eyes at this appeal, and the sternness of the officer was lost in the sensibility of the man.

"Don't you think, Lewtenant," he asked, "bein' as it's a *woman*—a *widder* woman too—the rules of war wouldn't be as severe on us for lettin' of her off, *purvidin*' she paid a reasonable fine?"

"They wouldn't be severe at all!" replied Snipes.

"Well, well, widder! Bein' as it's you—a perticlar friend and close neighbor—and bein' *as* you're a widder, and on the 'count of my feelins for Billy Haycock, which was your husband afore he died, I s'pose I'll have to run the resk. But it's a orful 'sponsibility I'm a-takin, jist for friend*ship*, widder—"

Mrs. Haycock interrupted him with a torrent of thanks and benedictions.

"Thar aint *many*," continued Suggs, "I'd take sich a 'sponsibility for: I may be a-runnin of *my own neck* into a halter!"

"The Lord in Heaven purvent your ever sufferin' bekase you've tuk pity on a poor widder like me!" was the grateful woman's ejaculation.

"Hows'ever," added Suggs, "to shorten the matter, jist pay down twenty-five dollars, and I'll pardon you ef I *do* git into a scrape about it—I never *could* bar to see a woman suffer! it strikes me right *here!*" and the Captain placed his hand upon his breast in a most impressive manner.

The joyful Mrs. Haycock immediately untied a key from her girdle, and handing it to one of her friends, sent her into the store, with directions "to sarch low down, in the left hand corner before of her chist," and bring a certain stocking she would find there filled with coin. This was speedily done, and the amount of the fine handed to Captain Suggs.

"This here money," he remarked as he received it, "I want you all to onderstand, aint *my* money. No! no! I have to keep it here"—sliding it into his pockets—"ontwell I git *my* orders about it. It's the *government's* money, and *I* darsent spend a cent of it —do I, Lewtenant?"

"No more'n you dar to put your head in a blazin' log-pile!" answered the Lieutenant.

A whistling—just such as always implies that somebody, in the immediate neighbourhood of the whistler, *lies tremendously*—was heard at this moment, and Suggs looking round, saw Yellow-legs in his old corner, dealing a supposititious hand of cards to an imaginary antagonist—as if he would thereby intimate that Captain Simon Suggs would embezzle the public money, or at any rate, hazard its loss at cards

"Charge baggonets on that cussed, pumkin-faced whelp of the devil!" roared the Captain in the phrensy of the moment; and Lieutenant Snipes dashed at Yellow-legs with his rusty weapon, which he plunged through a crack of the fence! Before the gallant Snipes, however, could recover from the impetus of his attack and withdraw the bayonet, the dirt-eater had pulled it off the hoe-handle, and fixing it on a dry corn-stalk, bore it aloft upon his shoulder most contumaciously, under the very nose of Captain Suggs!

* * * * * *

The reader will please suppose fifteen minutes to have elapsed, and Captain Suggs and his Lieutenant to be behind the store chimney, in private conversation.

"Lewtenant Snipes!" said Suggs, "I look upon you as a high-minded, honubble officer, and a honor to the Tallapoosy Vollantares. I like to see a man do his duty like you done *yourn!* Here, take *that!*"—handing him one of Mrs. Haycock's dollars—"Simon Suggs never forgits his friends—NEVER! His motter is allers, *Fust* his *country,* and *then* his *friends!*"

"Capting Suggs"—was the Lieutenant's reply, as he made a minute examination of the Mexican coin in his hand—"I've said it *behind you back,* and I'll say it *to you're face;* you're a *gentleman* from the top of your head to the end of your big-toe nail! Less go in and liquor; damn expenses!"

CHAPTER THE NINTH.

THE " TALLAPOOSY VOLLANTARES" MEET THE ENEMY.

CAPTAIN SUGGS, with the troops under his command, remained, we believe, during the entire continuance of the " war," in garrison at the Fort. The reason for this was obvious. The object of our hero was to protect that portion of the country which had the strongest claims upon his affection—his own neighbourhood. It was beyond human knowledge to foretell how soon the wily savage might raise the tomahawk and scalping knife in the immediate vicinity of Fort Suggs. Why then should any body ever have expected, or desired the Captain to leave that important post and the circumjacent country in a state of absolute defencelessness? Suggs was too prudent for that: he remained snug enough at the Fort, subsisting comfortably upon the contributions which he almost daily levied from wagons passing with flour, bacon, and whiskey, from Wetumpka eastward. In his own energetic language, " he had tuk his persition, and d—d ef he didn't keep it as long as he had yeath enough to stand upon!"

In spite of the excitement of frequent *sorties* upon ox-wagons; of dollar-pitching, and an endless series of games of " old sledge;" as well as the occasional exhibition of a chuck-a-luck table, at which the Captain himself presided; time at last began to hang heavily upon the hands of the inmates of Fort Suggs.

At length, however, an event occurred which dis-
pelled the *ennui* of the "Vollantares," for a season
at least. An Indian *ball-play* was announced to
"come off" within a few days, at the ball-ground
near the river, and only three miles from the fort,
though on the opposite side of the Tallapoosa. It
was decided that Captain Suggs and his company
should attend and witness the sport; and as both the
towns engaged in the game were reputed to be
"friendly," not the slightest danger was anticipated.
Had there been, from our knowledge of the prudence
of Captain Suggs, we do not hesitate to say, that he
would never have jeoparded his own invaluable life,
not to speak of those of his comparatively insignifi-
cant soldiers, by appearing on the ball-ground. Tiresome as was the monotony of Fort Suggs, he would
have remained there indefinitely, ere he had done
his country such wrong!

Early on the day appointed for the trial of skill between the copper-coloured sportsmen of the towns of
Upper and Lower Oakfuskee, the "Vollantares" and
their illustrious Captain had crossed the river at the
ferry which lay between the fort and the ball-ground,
and soon they had reached the long, straight pine
ridge upon which the game was to be played. Already two or three hundred Indians had assembled, and the Captain also found there some ten or a
dozen white men. A stake was set up close to the
goal which was nearest the river, and from its top
hung a huge shot-bag of crimson cloth, covered with
beautiful bead-work, and filled with the silver money
which was bet on the result of the game. At the

foot of the stake, on the ground, were blankets, shawls, guns, bolts of cotton goods, and all sorts of trumpery; all of which was also bet on the result. The "odds" were in favour of the Lower Oakfuskees, among whom were some of the best players in the "nation," and Captain Suggs quickly backed them to the amount of ten dollars, and the money was added to that already in the shot-pouch.

The Indian game of ball is a very exciting one, and the Creeks gamble furiously at it. To play it, a level piece of ground, some two or three hundred yards long, is selected, and the centre ascertained. Goals are designated at each end, and the ball—very like that used in games among the whites, but not so elastic—is thrown up at the centre. One side endeavours to get it to one "base," while their antagonists strive to carry it to the other. The players are armed with two short sticks, each of which is bent and tied at one end, so as to form a sort of spoon; and when these ends are placed together they make an oval cup in which the ball is caught, and then hurled to a surprising distance. Every time the ball is carried to a goal, it counts one for the side who take it there. No idea of the furious excitement into which the players are worked, can be conceived by one who has never witnessed a scene of the kind. They run over and trample upon each other; knock down their antagonists with their ball-sticks; trip them as they are running at full speed; and, in short, employ all kinds of force and foul playing to win the game. Generally there are two or three hundred—often five—engaged in the sport at once; all naked except the "flap," and

in most instances the affair ends in a terrible *melée*,
in which the squaws on each side supply their male
friends with missiles, such as rocks and light-wood
knots.   The betting is often high; the main bet being, not uncommonly, five hundred dollars.

On the present occasion the game was "twenty-one
up."   The playing commenced, and the woods re-
sounded with the fierce yells of the naked savages.
The first run was gained by the upper town, but the
next, and the next, and the next, were won with ease
by the lower.   The Captain was exultant, and
whooped loudly at every winning.

At length, when it was seen that the upper town
must lose, one of the white men whom Captain Suggs
found on the ground when he arrived—and who was
the heaviest better against the lower town—approached our hero, and informed him that he had discovered the astounding fact, that both parties of Indians were determined to make a sudden attack upon
all the white men present, and kill them to a man.
He stated farther, that he had overheard a conversation between Cocher-Emartee, the chief of the upper
town, and Nocose Harjo, the principal man of the
lower, in which it was agreed between them, that the
signal for attack should be the throwing of the ball
straight up into the air.   In view of these facts, he
advised the Captain to leave at once, whenever he
should see the signal given.

Captain Suggs is human, and " *as sich*" is liable
to err, but it isn't *often* that he can be "throwed" by
ordinary men.   He " saw through the trap" that was
set for him in a minute.   He did not doubt that an

attack would be made, he knew that a *feigned* one would be made by Cocher-Emartee's Indians, and he was well convinced that its only object would be to frighten the " Vollantares" from the ground, and give the upper town an opportunity, with the assistance of their white confederates, to beat the lower town Indians and seize the stakes. He determined therefore to " watch out," and keep himself " whole" in a pecuniary point of view if possible. Calling his trusty lieutenant to his side, he discovered to him the machinations against them, and directing him to keep the company—most of whom were a-foot—in the neighbourhood of a number of ponies that were hitched near the upper end of the ball-ground; he himself walked to the lower end, and bringing his pony close to the post from which the shot-pouch was suspended, he hitched him and sat down.

Suddenly, when most of the Indians were collected near the centre of the ground, the ball was seen to ascend high into the air. Simon was watching for it, and before it had risen twenty feet, had loosed his pony, flung the reins over his neck, cracked him smartly across the rump, and so started him home by himself. The next moment he was mounted on a fine blood bay, belonging to Cocher-Emartee, which wheeling under the post, he took off the shot-bag containing the stakes with the muzzle of his rifle, and in less time than we have taken to describe his movements, was thundering at full speed through the woods towards the ferry, the silver in the pouch giving a responsive jingle to every bound of the gallant bay.

K

At the same moment that Captain Suggs mounted and dashed off, most of the " Vollantares," under the lead of Snipes, jumped upon the ponies of the upper Oakfuskees and made for the river. A volley of rifle shots was discharged over their heads, and with furious yells the Indians pursued. Only a few, however, could muster ponies; and such was the promptness with which the Captain's orders were executed, that the " Vollantares " arrived at the ferry full five minutes in advance of their pursuers. Here a difficulty presented itself. The flat would not carry across more than a fourth of the company at once. Time was precious—the enemy was rushing onward, now fully determined to recover their ponies or die in the attempt. Suggs, equal to any emergency, cut loose the flat and started it down the river. Then holding his gun aloft, he dashed his spurs into his horse's flanks and plunged into the stream, and his men followed. As they ascended the opposite bank, Cocher-Emartee, foaming and furious, rode up on the side they had just left. He was mounted on a borrowed horse, and now loudly howled forth his demand for the restoration of his gallant bay and the shot-bag of silver; protesting that the whole affair was a joke on his part to try the spunk of the " Vollantares "— that he was " good friends " to the white people, and didn't wish to injure any of them.

"Go to h–ll! you d—d old bandy-shanked redskin!" shouted back Simon; " I know the inemies of my country better'n that!"

Cocher danced, shouted, raved, bellowed, and snorted in his boundless rage! Finally, he urged his pony into the water with the intention of swimming across.

"Kumpny form!" shouted Simon—"blaze away at the d—d old *hostile!*" A volley was fired, and when the smoke cleared away, the pony was seen struggling in the river, but there were no Indians in sight.

Captain Suggs never recovered the pony which he turned loose in the woods; and notwithstanding this loss was incurred while in the discharge of his duties as one of the defenders of his country, the state legislature has *thrice* refused to grant him any remuneration whatsoever. Truly " republics *are* ungrateful!"

CHAPTER THE TENTH.

THE CAPTAIN ATTENDS A CAMP-MEETING.

CAPTAIN SUGGS found himself as poor at the conclusion of the Creek war, as he had been at its commencement. Although no "arbitrary," "despotic," "corrupt," and "unprincipled" judge had fined him a thousand dollars for his proclamation of martial law at Fort Suggs, or the enforcement of its rules in the case of Mrs. Haycock; yet somehow—the thing is alike inexplicable to him and to us—the money which he had contrived, by various shifts to obtain, melted away and was gone for ever. To a man like the Captain, of intense domestic affections, this state of destitution was most distressing. "He could stand it himself—didn't care a d—n for it, no way," he observed, "but the old woman and the children; *that* bothered him!"

As he sat one day, ruminating upon the unpleasant condition of his "financial concerns," Mrs. Suggs informed him that "the sugar and coffee was nigh about out," and that there were not "a dozen j'ints and middlins, *all put together*, in the smoke-house." Suggs bounced up on the instant, exclaiming, "D—n it! *somebody* must suffer!" But whether this remark was intended to convey the idea that he and his family were about to experience the want of the necessaries of life; or that some other, and as yet unknown individual should "suffer" to prevent that prospec-

tive exigency, must be left to the commentators, if
perchance any of that ingenious class of persons
should hereafter see proper to write notes for this history. It is enough for us that we give all the facts
in this connection, so that ignorance of the subsequent
conduct of Captain Suggs may not lead to an errone-
ous judgment in respect to his words.

Having uttered the exclamation we have repeated
—and perhaps, hurriedly walked once or twice across
the room—Captain Suggs drew on his famous old
green-blanket overcoat, and ordered his horse, and
within five minutes was on his way to a camp-meeting, then in full blast on Sandy creek, twenty miles
distant, where he hoped to find amusement, at least.
When he arrived there, he found the hollow square
of the encampment filled with people, listening to the
mid-day sermon and its dozen accompanying "ex-
hortations." A half-dozen preachers were dispensing
the word; the one in the pulpit, a meek-faced old
man, of great simplicity and benevolence. His voice
was weak and cracked, notwithstanding which, however, he contrived to make himself heard occasionally, above the din of the exhorting, the singing, and
the shouting which were going on around him. The
rest were walking to and fro, (engaged in the other
exercises we have indicated,) among the "mourners"—a host of whom occupied the seat set apart for
their especial use—or made personal appeals to the
mere spectators. The excitement was intense. Men
and women rolled about on the ground, or lay sobbing or shouting in promiscuous heaps. More than
all, the negroes sang and screamed and prayed. Se-

veral, under the influence of what is technically called
"the jerks," were plunging and pitching about with
convulsive energy. The great object of all seemed
to be, to see who could make the greatest noise—

> "And each—for madness ruled the hour—
>   Would try his own expressive power."

"Bless my poor old soul!" screamed the preacher
in the pulpit; "ef yonder aint a squad in that corner
that we aint got one outen yet! It'll never do"—
raising his voice—"you must come outen that!
Brother Fant, fetch up that youngster in the blue
coat! I see the Lord's a-workin' upon him! Fetch
him along—glory—yes!—hold to him!"

"Keep the thing warm!" roared a sensual seeming man, of stout mould and florid countenance, who
was exhorting among a bevy of young women, upon
whom he was lavishing caresses. "Keep the thing
warm, breethring!—come to the Lord, honey!" he
added, as he vigorously hugged one of the damsels
he sought to save.

"Oh, I've got him!" said another in exulting
tones, as he led up a gawky youth among the mourners—"I've got him—he tried to git off, but—ha!
Lord!"—shaking his head as much as to say, it took
a smart fellow to escape him—"ha! Lord!"—and
he wiped the perspiration from his face with one
hand, and with the other, patted his neophyte on the
shoulder—"he couldn't do it! No! Then he tried
to argy wi' me—but bless the Lord!—he couldn't do
that nother! Ha! Lord! I tuk him, fust in the Old
Testament—bless the Lord!—and I argyed him all

thro' Kings—then I throwed him into Proverbs!—
and from that, here we had it up and down, kleer
down to the New Testament, and then I begun to see
it work him!—then we got into Matthy, and from
Matthy right straight along to Acts; and *thar* I
throwed him! Y–e–s L–o–r–d!"—assuming the
nasal twang and high pitch which are, in some parts,
considered the perfection of rhetorical art—"Y–e–s
L–o–r–d! and h–e–r–e he is! Now g–i–t down
thar," addressing the subject, "and s–e–e ef the
L–o–r–d won't do somethin' f–o–r you!" Having
thus deposited his charge among the mourners, he
started out, summarily to convert another soul!

"Gl–o–*ree!*" yelled a huge, greasy negro woman,
as in a fit of the jerks, she threw herself convulsively
from her feet, and fell "like a thousand of brick,"
across a diminutive old man in a little round hat,
who was squeaking consolation to one of the
mourners.

"Good Lord, have mercy!" ejaculated the little
man earnestly and unaffectedly, as he strove to crawl
from under the sable mass which was crushing him.

In another part of the square a dozen old women
were singing. They were in a state of absolute ex-
tasy, as their shrill pipes gave forth,

> "I rode on the sky,
>   Quite ondestified I,
> And the moon it was under my feet!"

Near these last, stood a delicate woman in that
hysterical condition in which the nerves are incon-
trollable, and which is vulgarly—and almost blas-

phemously—termed the "holy laugh." A hideous grin distorted her mouth, and was accompanied with a maniac's chuckle; while every muscle and nerve of her face twitched and jerked in horrible spasms.*

Amid all this confusion and excitement Suggs stood unmoved. He viewed the whole affair as a grand deception—a sort of "opposition line" running against his own, and looked on with a sort of professional jealousy. Sometimes he would mutter running comments upon what passed before him.

"Well now," said he, as he observed the full-faced brother who was "officiating" among the women, "that ere feller takes *my* eye!—thar he's een this half-hour, a-figurin amongst them galls, and's never said the fust word to nobody else. Wonder what's the reason these here preachers never hugs up the old, ugly women? Never seed one do it in my life—the sperrit never moves 'em that way! It's nater tho'; and the women, *they* never flocks round one o' the old dried-up breethring—bet two to one old splinter-legs thar,"—nodding at one of the ministers—" won't git a chance to say turkey to a good-

---

* The reader is requested to bear in mind, that the scenes described in this chapter are not *now* to be witnessed. Eight or ten years ago, all classes of population of the Creek country were very different from what they now are. Of course, no disrespect is intended to any denomination of Christians. We believe that camp-meetings are not peculiar to any church, though most usual in the Methodist—a denomination whose respectability in Alabama is attested by the fact, that *very many* of its worthy clergymen and lay members. hold honourable and profitable offices in the gift of the state legislature; of which, indeed, almost a controlling portion are themselves Methodists

lookin gall to-day! Well! who blames 'em? Nater
will be nater, all the world over; and I judge ef I
was a preacher, I should save the purtiest souls fust,
myself!"

While the Captain was in the middle of this conversation with himself, he caught the attention of the
preacher in the pulpit, who inferring from an indescribable something about his appearance that he was
a person of some consequence, immediately determined to add him at once to the church if it could be
done; and to that end began a vigorous, direct personal attack.

"Breethring," he exclaimed, "I see yonder a
man that's a sinner; I _know_ he's a sinner! Thar he
stands," pointing at Simon, " a missubble old crittur,
with his head a-blossomin for the grave! A few
more short years, and d--o--w--n he'll go to perdition,
lessen the Lord have mer--cy on him! Come up
here, you old hoary-headed sinner, a--n--d git down
upon your knees, a--n--d put up your cry for the Lord
to snatch you from the bottomless pit! You're ripe
for the devil—you're b--o--u--n--d for hell, and the
Lord only knows what'll become on you!"

"D—n it," thought Suggs, "_ef_ I only had you
down in the krick swamp for a minit or so, _I'd_ show
you who's _old! I'd_ alter your tune _mighty_ sudden,
you sassy, 'saitful old rascal!" But he judiciously
held his tongue and gave no utterance to the thought.

The attention of many having been directed to the
Captain by the preacher's remarks, he was soon surrounded by numerous well-meaning, and doubtless
very pious persons, each one of whom seemed bent

on the application of his own particular recipe for the salvation of souls. For a long time the Captain stood silent, or answered the incessant stream of exhortation only with a sneer ; but at length, his countenance began to give token of inward emotion. First his eye-lids twitched—then his upper lip quivered—next a transparent drop formed on one of his eye-lashes, and a similar one on the tip of his nose—and, at last, a sudden bursting of air from nose and mouth, told that Captain Suggs was overpowered by his emotions. At the moment of the explosion, he made a feint as if to rush from the crowd, but he was in experienced hands, who well knew that the battle was more than half won.

"Hold to him !" said one—"it's a-workin in him as strong as a Dick horse !"

"Pour it into him," said another, "it'll all come right directly !"

"That's the way I love to see 'em do," observed a third ; when you begin to draw the water from their eyes, taint gwine to be long afore you'll have 'em on their knees !"

And so they clung to the Captain manfully, and half dragged, half led him to the mourner's bench ; by which he threw himself down, altogether unmanned, and bathed in tears. Great was the rejoicing of the brethren, as they sang, shouted, and prayed around him—for by this time it had come to be generally known that the "convicted" old man was Captain Simon Suggs, the very "chief of sinners" in all that region.

The Captain remained grovelling in the dust dur-

ing the usual time, and gave vent to even more than
the requisite number of sobs, and groans, and heart-
piercing cries. At length, when the proper time had
arrived, he bounced up, and with a face radiant with
joy, commenced a series of vaultings and tumblings,
which "laid in the shade" all previous performances
of the sort at that camp-meeting. The brethren were
in extasies at this demonstrative evidence of com-
pletion of the work; and whenever Suggs shouted
"Gloree!" at the top of his lungs, every one of them
shouted it back, until the woods rang with echoes.

The effervescence having partially subsided, Suggs
was put upon his pins to relate his experience, which
he did somewhat in this style—first brushing the
tear-drops from his eyes, and giving the end of his
nose a preparatory wring with his fingers, to free it
of the superabundant moisture :   ·

"Friends," he said, "it don't take long to curry
a short horse, accordin' to the old sayin', and I'll give
you the perticklers of the way I was 'brought to a
knowledge' "—here the Captain wiped his eyes,
brushed the tip of his nose and snuffled a little—"in
less'n no time."

"Praise the Lord!" ejaculated a bystander.

"You see I come here full o' romancin' and devilment, and jist to make game of all the purceedins.
Well, sure enough, I done so for some time, and was
a-thinkin how I should play some trick—" ·

"Dear soul alive! *don't* he talk sweet!" cried an
old lady in black silk—"Whar's John Dobbs? You
Sukey!" screaming at a negro woman on the other
side of the square—"ef you don't hunt up your mass

John in a minute, and have him here to listen to his 'sperience, I'll tuck you up when I git home and give you a hundred and fifty lashes, madam!—see ef I don't! Blessed Lord!"—referring again to the Captain's relation—"aint it a *precious* 'scource!"

"I was jist a-thinkin' how I should play some trick to turn it all into redecule, when they began to come round me and talk. Long at fust I didn't mind it, but arter a little that brother"—pointing to the reverend gentlemen who had so successfully carried the unbeliever through the Old and New Testaments, and who Simon was convinced was the " big dog of the tanyard"—"that brother spoke a word that struck me kleen to the heart, and run all over me, like fire in dry grass—"

" *I–I–I* can bring 'em!" cried the preacher alluded to, in a tone of exultation—"Lord thou knows ef thy servant can't stir 'em up, nobody else needn't try—but the glory aint mine! I'm a poor worrum of the dust" he added, with ill-managed affectation.

"And so from that I felt somethin' a-pullin' me inside—"

" Grace! grace! nothin' but grace!" exclaimed one; meaning that "grace" had been operating in the Captain's gastric region.

" And then," continued Suggs, " I wanted to git off, but they hilt me, and bimeby I felt so missuble, I had to go yonder"—pointing to the mourners' seat —"and when I lay down thar it got wuss and wuss, and 'peared like somethin' was a-mashin' down on my back—"

" That was his load o' sin," said one of the brethren—"never mind, it'll tumble off presently; see ef it don't!" and he shook his head professionally and knowingly.

"And it kept a-gittin heavier and heavier, ontwell it looked like it might be a four year old steer, or a big pine log, or somethin' of that sort—"

"Glory to my soul," shouted Mrs. Dobbs, "it's the sweetest talk I *ever* hearn! You Sukey! aint you got John yit? never mind, my lady, I'll settle wi' you!" Sukey quailed before the finger which her mistress shook at her.

"And arter awhile," Suggs went on, "'peared like I fell into a trance, like, and I seed—"

"Now we'll git the good on it!" cried one of the sanctified."

"And I seed the biggest, longest, rip-roarenest, blackest, scaliest—" Captain Suggs paused, wiped his brow, and ejaculated "Ah, L—o—r—d!" so as to give full time for curiosity to become impatience to know what he saw.

"*Sarpent!* warn't it?" asked one of the preachers.

"No, not a sarpent," replied Suggs, blowing his nose.

"Do tell us *what* it war, soul alive!—whar *is* John?" said Mrs. Dobbs.

"Allegator!" said the Captain.

"Alligator!" repeated every woman present, and screamed for very life.

Mrs. Dobb's nerves were so shaken by the announcement, that after repeating the horrible word, she screamed to Sukey, "you Sukey, I say, you Su—u—ke—e—y! ef you let John come a-nigh this way,

whar the dreadful alliga—shaw! what am I thinkin'
'bout? 'Twarn't nothin' but a vishin!"

" Well," said the Captain in continuation, "the
allegator kept a-comin' and a-comin' to'ards me, with
his great long jaws a-gapin' open like a ten-foot pair
o' tailors' shears—"

" Oh! oh! oh! Lord! gracious above!" cried the
women.

" SATAN!" was the laconic ejaculation of the old-
est preacher present, who thus informed the congregation that it was the devil which had attacked Suggs
in the shape of an alligator.

" And then I concluded the jig was up, 'thout I
could block his game some way; for I seed his idee
was to snap off my head—"

The women screamed again.

"So I fixed myself jist like I was purfectly willin'
for him to take my head, and rather he'd do it as
not"—here the women shuddered perceptibly—"and
so I hilt my head straight out"—the Captain illustrated by elongating his neck—" and when he come
up and was a gwine to *shet down* on it, I jist pitched
in a big rock which choked him to death, and that
minit I felt the weight slide off, and I had the best
feelins—sorter like you'll have from *good* sperrits—
any body ever had!"

" Didn't I *tell* you so? Didn't I *tell* you so?"
asked the brother who had predicted the off-tumbling
of the load of sin. " Ha, Lord! fool *who!* I've been
all along thar!—yes, *all along thar!* and I know
every inch of the way jist as good as I do the road
home!"—and then he turned round and round, and

looked at all, to receive a silent tribute to his superior penetration.

Captain Suggs was now the "lion of the day."
Nobody could pray so well, or exhort so movingly,
as "brother Suggs." Nor did his natural modesty
prevent the proper performance of appropriate exercises. With the reverend Bela Bugg (him to whom,
under providence, he ascribed his conversion,) he
was a most especial favourite. They walked, sang,
and prayed together for hours.

"Come, come up; thar's room for all!" cried brother Bugg, in his evening exhortation. "Come to
the 'seat,' and ef you won't pray yourselves, let *me*
pray for you!"

"Yes!" said Simon, by way of assisting his
friend; "it's a game that all can win at! Ante up!
ante up, boys—friends I mean—don't back out!"

"Thar aint a sinner here," said Bugg, "no matter
ef his soul's black as a nigger, but what thar's room
for him!"

"No matter what sort of a hand you've got,"
added Simon in the fulness of his benevolence;
"take stock! Here am *I*, the wickedest and blind-
est of sinners—has spent my whole life in the sarvice
of the devil—has now come in on *narry pair* and
won a *pile!*" and the Captain's face beamed with
holy pleasure.

"D–o–n–'t be afeard!" cried the preacher; "come
along! the meanest won't be turned away! humble
yourselves and come!"

"No!" said Simon, still indulging in his favourite
style of metaphor; "the bluff game aint played here!

No runnin' of a body off! Every body holds four
aces, and when you bet, you win!"

And thus the Captain continued, until the services
were concluded, to assist in adding to the number at
the mourners' seat; and up to the hour of retiring, he
exhibited such enthusiasm in the cause, that he was
unanimously voted to be the most efficient addition
the church had made during that meeting.

The next morning, when the preacher of the day
first entered the pulpit, he announced that " brother
Simon Suggs," mourning over his past iniquities, and
desirous of going to work in the cause as speedily
as possible, would take up a collection to found
a church in his own neighbourhood, at which he
hoped to make himself useful as soon as he could
prepare himself for the ministry, which the preacher
didn't doubt, would be in a very few weeks, as brother Suggs was " a man of mighty good judgement,
and of *a great discorse.*" The funds were to be collected by " brother Suggs," and held in trust by brother Bela Bugg, who was the financial officer of the
circuit, until some arrangement could be made to
build a suitable house.

" Yes, breethring," said the Captain, rising to his
feet; " I want to start a little 'sociation close to me,
and I want you all to help. I'm mighty poor myself,
as poor as any of you—don't leave breethring"—ob-
serving that several of the well-to-do were about to
go off—" don't leave; ef you aint able to afford any
thing, jist give us your blessin' and it'll be all the
same!"

This insinuation did the business, and the sensitive individuals re-seated themselves.

"It's mighty little of this world's goods I've got," resumed Suggs, pulling off his hat and holding it before him; "but I'll bury *that* in the cause any how," and he deposited his last five-dollar bill in the hat.

There was a murmur of approbation at the Captain's liberality throughout the assembly.

Suggs now commenced collecting, and very prudently attacked first the gentlemen who had shown a disposition to escape. These, to exculpate themselves from any thing like poverty, contributed handsomely.

"Look here, breethring," said the Captain, displaying the bank-notes thus received, "brother Snooks has drapt a five wi' me, and brother Snodgrass a ten! In course 'taint expected that you *that aint as well off as them*, will give *as much;* let every one give *accordin'* to ther means."

This was another chain-shot that raked as it went! "Who so low" as not to be able to contribute as much as Snooks and Snodgrass?

"Here's all the *small* money I've got about me," said a burly old fellow, ostentatiously handing to Suggs, over the heads of a half dozen, a ten dollar bill.

"That's what I call maganimus!" exclaimed the Captain; "that's the way *every* rich man ought to do!"

These examples were followed, more or less closely, by almost all present, for Simon had excited the pride of purse of the congregation, and a

very handsome sum was collected in a very short
time.

The reverend Mr. Bugg, as soon as he observed
that our hero had obtained all that was to be had at
that time, went to him and inquired what amount had
been collected.   The Captain replied that it was still
uncounted, but that it couldn't be much under a
hundred.

" Well, brother Suggs, you'd better count it and
turn it over to me now.   I'm goin' to leave presently."

" No!" said Suggs—" can't do it!"

" Why ?—what's the matter ?" inquired Bugg.

" It's got to be *prayed over*, fust!" said Simon, a
heavenly smile illuminating his whole face.

" Well," replied Bugg, " less go one side and do
it !"

" No!" said Simon, solemnly.

Mr. Bugg gave a look of inquiry.

"You see that krick swamp ?" asked Suggs—
" I'm gwine down in *thar*, and I'd gwine to lay this
money down *so*"—showing how he would place it
on the ground—" and I'm gwine to git on these here
knees"—slapping the right one—" and I'm n-e-v-e-r
gwine to quit the grit ontwell I feel it's got the
blessin' !   And   nobody   aint   got   to   be   thar   but
me !"

Mr. Bugg greatly admired the Captain's fervent
piety, and bidding him God-speed, turned off.

Captain Suggs " struck for" the swamp sure
enough, where his horse was already hitched.   " Ef

them fellers aint done to a cracklin," he muttered to himself as he mounted, " *I*'ll never bet on two pair agin! They're peart at the snap game, theyselves; but they're badly lewed this hitch! Well! Live and let live is a good old motter, and it's my sentiments adzactly!" And giving the spur to his horse, off he cantered.

CHAPTER THE ELEVENTH.

THE CAPTAIN IS ARRAIGNED BEFORE "A JURY OF HIS COUNTRY."

FOR a year or two after the Captain's conversion at the camp-meeting, the memoranda at our command furnish no information concerning him. We next find him, at the spring term 1838, arraigned in the circuit court for the county of Tallapoosa, charged in a bill of indictment with gambling—"playing at a certain game of cards, commonly called *Poker*, for money, contrary to the form of the statute, and against the peace and dignity of the state of Alabama."

"Humph!" said the Captain to himself, as Mr. Solicitor Belcher read the bill; "*that's* as derned a lie as ever Jim Belcher writ! Thar never were a *peaceabler* or more *gentlemanlier* game o' short cards played in Datesville—which thar's a dozen men here is knowin' to it!"

Captain Suggs had no particular defence with which to meet the prosecution. It was pretty generally understood that the state would make out a pretty clear case against him; and a considerable fine —or imprisonment in default of its payment—was the certainly expected result. Yet Simon had employed —though he had not actually *feed*—counsel, and had some slight hope that LUCK, the goddess of his especial adoration, would not desert him at the pinch.

He instructed his lawyer, therefore, to stave off the case if possible; or at any rate, to protract it.

"The State against Simon Suggs and Andrew alias Andy, Owens. Card-playing. Hadenskeldt for the defence. Are the defendants in court?" said the judge.

Simon's counsel intimated that *he* was.

"Take an *alias* writ as to Owens—ready for trial as to Suggs;" said the solicitor.

The Captain whispered to his lawyer, and urged him to put him on the stand, and make a showing for a continuance; but being advised by that gentleman that it would be useless, got him to obtain leave for him to go out of court for five minutes. Permission obtained, he went out and soon after returned.

"Is Wat Craddock in court?" asked the solicitor.

"Here!" said Wat.

"Take the stand, Mr. Craddock!" and Wat obeyed and was sworn.

"Proceed, Mr. Craddock, and tell the court and jury all you know about Captain Suggs' playing cards," said Mr. Belcher.

"Stop!" interposed Simon's counsel; "do you believe in the revelations of Scripture, Mr. Craddock?"

"No!" said the witness.

"I object then to his testifying," said Mr. Hadenskeldt.——— — - -

"He doesn't *understand the question*," said the solicitor; "you believe the Bible to be true, don't you?" addressing the witness.

"If the court please—stop! *stop!* Mr. Craddock— I'll ask him another question before he answers that"

—said Mr. Hadenskeldt hastily—" did you ever *read* the Bible, Mr. Craddock?"

" No," said Craddock; " not's I know on."

" Then I object to his testifying, of course; he can't believe what he knows nothing about."

" He has *heard* it read, I presume," said Mr. Belcher; " have you not, Mr. Craddock?"

" I mought," said Wat, " but I don't know."

" *Don't know!* Why, don't you hear it every Sunday at church?"

" Ah, but you see," replied Mr. Craddock, with the air of a man about to solve a difficulty to every body's satisfaction—" You see, I don't never go to meetin!"

" Your honor will perceive—" began Mr. Hadenskeldt.

" Why—what—how do you spend your time on Sunday, Mr. Craddock?" asked the solicitor.

" Sometimes I goes a-fishin on the krick, and sometimes I plays marvels," replied Wat, gaping extensively as he spoke.

" Any thing else?"

" Sometimes I lays in the sun, back o' Andy Owenses grocery."

" Mr. Belcher," asked the court, " is this the only witness for the state?"

" We have a half-dozen more who can prove all the facts?"

" Well then, discharge this man—he's drunk."

Mr. Craddock was accordingly discharged, and William Sentell was put upon the stand. Just as he had kissed the book, a man, looking hot and worried, was seen leaning over the railing which shuts out the spectators from the business part of the court-room, beckoning to the Captain.

Simon having obtained leave to see this person, went to him, and took a note which the other held in his hand, and after a few words of conversation, turned off to read it. As he slowly deciphered the words, his countenance changed and he began to weep. The solicitor, who knew a thing or two about the Captain, laughed; and so did Mr. Hadenskeldt, although he tried to suppress it.

"My boys is a-dyin!" said Suggs; and he threw himself upon the steps leading to the judge's seat, and sobbed bitterly.

"Come, come, Captain," said the solicitor; "you *are* a great tactician, but permit me to say that *I* know you. Come, no shamming; let's proceed with the trial."

"It don't make no odds to me now, what you do about it—John and Ben will be in ther graves before I git home;" and the poor fellow groaned heart-breakingly.

"Captain," said Mr. Hadenskeldt, vainly endeavouring to control his risibles, "let us attend to the trial now: may be it isn't as bad as you suppose."

"No," said Suggs, "let 'em find me guilty. I'm a poor missuble old man! The Lord's a-punishin my gray hairs for my wickedness!"

Mr. Hadenskeldt took from the Captain's hand the note containing the bad tidings, and to his great astonishment saw that it was from Dr. Jourdan, a gentleman well known to him, and entirely above any suspicion of trickery. It set forth that the Captain's sons were at the point of death—one of them beyond hope; and urged the Captain to come home to his afflicted family. Knowing that Suggs was really an affectionate father, he was now at no loss to account for the naturalness of his grief, which he had before supposed to be simulated. He instantly read the note aloud, and remarked that he would throw himself upon the humanity of the state's counsel for a continuance.

Simon interposed—"Never mind," he sobbed, "'squire Hadenskeldt—never mind—let 'em try me. I'll plead guilty. The boys will be dead afore I could git home any how! Let 'em send me to jail whar thar won't be any body to laugh at my misry!"

"Has this poor old man ever been indicted before?" asked the judge.

"Never," said the solicitor, who was affected almost to tears—"he has the reputation of being dissipated and tricky, but I think has never been in court, at the instance of the state, before."

"Ah, well then, Mr. Belcher," replied the judge, "I would 'nol. pros.' the case, if I were you, and let this grief-stricken old man go home to his dying children. He is indicted only for a misdemeanour, and it would be absolute inhumanity to keep him here; perhaps that lenity might have a good effect, too."

This was all the solicitor wished for. He was already burning to strike the case off the docket, and send Simon home; for he was one of the men that could never look real grief in the face, without a tear in his eye—albeit his manner was as rough as a Russian bear's.

So the solicitor entered his *nolle prosequi*, and the Captain was informed that he was at liberty.

"May it please your honor, judge," said he, picking up his hat, "and all you other kind gentlemen"—his case had excited universal commiseration among the lawyers—"that's taken pity on a poor broken-sperrited man—God bless you all for it—it's all I can say or do!" He then left the court-house.

In the course of an hour or two, the solicitor had occasion to go to his room for a paper or book he had left there. On his way to the tavern, he observed Captain Suggs standing in front of a "grocery," in great glee, relating some laughable anecdote. He was astounded! He called to him, and the Captain came.

"Captain Suggs," said the solicitor, "how's this? Why are you not on the way home?" And the solicitor frowned like—as only *he can* frown.

"Why bless my soul, Jim," said Suggs familiarly, and with a wicked smile, "aint you *hearn* about it? These here boys in town"—here *Simon* himself frowned savagely—I'll be d—d in*to* an *orful* h–ll, ef I don't knock daylight outen some on 'em—*a-sportin wi' my feelins*, that way! They'd better mind—jokin's jokin, but I've known men most hellatiously *kicked* for jist sich jokes!"

"Well, well," said Mr. Belcher, who more than suspected that he had been "sold"—"how was it?"

"You see," quoth Simon, "it was this here way, adzactly—that note I got in the court-house, was one

M

Dr. Jourdan sent me last summer, when the boys *was* sick, and I was on a spree over to Sockapatoy—only *I* didn't know 'twas the same. It must 'a drapped outen my pocket here, somehow, and some of these cussed town boys picked it up, tore off the date at the bottom, and sent it to me up thar—which, my feelins was never hurt as bad before, in the round world. But they'd *better mind* who they poke thar fun at! *No-o* man aint got to sport wi' *my* feelins that way, and let me find him out!—Won't you take some sperrits, Jim?"

The solicitor turned off wrathfully, and walked away. Simon watched him as he went. "Thar," said he, "goes as clever a feller as ever toted a ugly head! He's *smart* too—d—d smart; but thar's *some* people he can't qu—u—i—te, ad—zact—ly—" and without finishing the sentence, Captain Suggs pulled down the lower lid of his left eye, with the forefinger of his right hand; and having thus impliedly complimented himself, he walked back to the grocery.

CHAPTER THE TWELFTH.

CONCLUSION—AUTOGRAPHIC LETTER FROM SUGGS.

WE were just about penning some brief words, by way of conclusion, when there was handed to us a letter bearing the superscription, " to the edditur of the eest Allybammyun, la Fait, chambers Kounty, Al." It was from Suggs. We here present it to our readers, premising that with the exception of the punctuation, which we have altered—or rather added—it is a faithful transcript:

" Der Johns—Arter my kompliments, &c. I set down to rite you a fu lines consarin of them hoss papers" (the Captain alludes to the New York Spirit of the Times) " you had sent to me from the norrud, which I'm much ableeged for the same, and you kin tell the printer to keep a-sendin as long as he wants to. The picters is great. That wun bout me and Bill and old Jediar," (Suggs speaks of an illustration, published in advance in the " Spirit," intended for Mr. Porter's volume, entitled " The Big Bear of Arkansas and other Sketches,") " I faults in only wun purtickler—it's got a punchun fence in the place of a rale one—which I never seed a punchun fence in my life exsept round a garding. Thar is a thing 'sprises me mightly; how in life did the feller as drawd that picter ever see Bill, which has been ded the rise of twenty year? I kin see how he got *my* feeturs on the count of your sendin of 'em on; but Bill's what bothers me! And thar he is, in the picter, with more giniwine nigger in him an you'll find nowadaze in a whole korn-field—owin to the breed bein so devilishly mixed. That uther picter," (intended also for Mr. Porter's volume,) "bout the feller swallerin the aushter, kums nigher draggin the bush up by the roots an a most enny thing I ever seed. Couldn't you git the printer to make me wun jist like it, only about 4 foot squar?" (Can you, Mr. Darley?)

"Oh Johns, don't you mind what the boys tells you bout my bein mad on the count of your ritin bout me. You mind they had jist sich a lie out bout me and Charly McL——e—which thar come d—d nigh bein gallons of blood drawd about it. I nevver wus mad, only sed I should be ef you rit that story bout the muscadine vine on the river, which I wouldn't care a dried-apple d—m for 'the boys' to know it, only the old woman would be shure to hear bout it, and then the yeath would shake! Wimmin is a monstus jellus thing.

"In the place of that air story consarnin of the muscadines, I'il give you a itum bout the way I sarved that swindlin missheen they had in Wetumpky, that they kalled the Wetumpky Tradin Kumpiny; which, you bein of a brittish feddul edditur—and usetur to be as nisey a dimmikrat as ever drinkt whiskey, more's yer shame now—you kin fix it up to the best advantedge." (Tell your own story, Capting!)

"You see I was thar bout the time The thing started, and they hadn't more'n got out bills enuf to shingle a small sized fire-proof war-house, and they

wanted to git out a few more. So they comes to me
—see, they'd *hearn* I was smart for a feller as had no
eddication—and ses old Chamblin, which were the
prezzident, ses he, capting Suggs, we've onderstood
you're a gentleman of great feenanshul abillitys, and
the institushun would be glad to have your sarvices
in gittin of its notes inter surkilashun. I knowd in a
minnit what he was up to; so I tetched my hat to
him, and ses I, tell the institushun I'll be very happy
to do what I kin, purvidin it pays me for the trouble.
Well, we argied it all over, and at last they agrees
to give me $2000 dollars in *thar* bills, to go out wun
month and buy niggars for 'em with thar money.
But fust, you see, they interduces me to a mister
Smith, and ses old Chamblin, ses he, capting Suggs,
our *friend*, mister Smith, will meet you by *axident* in
Urwintun, and sell you too or three niggars for our
notes—you onderstand—jist to *start* the thing. And
then the old feller made monkey moshins to let me
know twas to be a *sham* sale to git other people to
sell for the same money—which I seed inter the thing
from the jump. I didn't say nuthin, but jist batted
my eye at old Chamblin, and he laffed; and mister
Smith said *he* was willin to sell for that sort of money,
for he looked on the institushun as bein the most the
saulventest in the stait.

Well, they gin me my $2000 dollars to itself, and
then they krammed my ole saddel baggs as full as
they'd hold of thar bills, and I maid a brake on a
bee line for Urwinton. Thar I gin out I wanted to
buy niggars to stock my plantashun; but people sed
my money was too nu and too much of a kind. So

I couldn't buy none. Bimeby mister Smith he come along, and *he* wouldn't have nothin *but* Tradin Kumpany money for *his* niggers. Well, we happened together in the biggest crowd we could find, and struk up a trade *directly*. He had a kupple of mighty likely nigger fellers, and I gin him $1100 dollars for the two. Still, somehow or another, the fish *wouldn't* bite! Peeple had tuk a distaist to the money, and exsept a $100 dollers I paid my tavurn bill with, and $500 dollers I anteed off amongst the boys of a night, I couldn't git off a sent. From that I tuk off, all over the kuntry, and tried my d—dst, but it *wouldn't* grind no way you could let the water on it. So at the eend of the month, I got back home, and hadn't been thar long afore old Chamblin come up for a settle*ment*. I soon told him how the thing stood, and axed him to take back his d—d old bills, for peeple shunned 'em like the small-pox: even the niggers knowd they warn't no 'count. The ole feller looked as pided as a rattle-snaik, I tell you! Well, ses he, what did you do with Smith's niggers? Sold 'em, ses I. Ah, ses he, you ortent to a done that—what did you git for 'em? A thousen dollers, ses I, in stait money. Purty good, ses he—purty good!—see they warn't wuth more'n that. Well, ses he, you'd better giv me the money and let me reseet you— we're wantin stait funds down at the institushun mightily. I *reckon* not, ses I. WH-A-T! ses he. Ses I, I bought them niggers *with my own funds which you paid me*; and, ses I, its mighty well I got off part of my money that way, or I should a' lost it *all*, ses I. *Then* he snorted! You're a swindler,

I rolled up my shirt-sleeves—which it was tollable warm day and my boat was out—and so I says you see that boss yonder

ses he! How? ses I. Them niggers b'longed to the institushun, ses he, and Smith was only *agent*. Well, ses I, didn't I pay the agent of the institushun $1100 dollers for 'em? ses I. Call *that* swindlin? ses I. Paid 'em in *ther own paper* too! ses I. Well, that sorter stumped him, but he kep up a h—ll of a *growlin*, ontwell at last, finally, I rolled up my shirt sleeves —which it was a tolluble warm day and my koat was off—and ses I, you see that hoss yonder? ses I. Yes, ses he. It's *your* hoss, aint it? ses I. Yes, ses he. Well, ses I, ef you don't want to be eet up boddaciously, ses I, you'd better git a-top of him and slope! and I gin him the sivvairest look *he* ever seed. Sure enut, he tuk me at my word, and I aint hearn from him nor his d—d rotten institushun sense!

When you come over to cort, Johns, I want you to tch me a kupple of packs of the dokkyments—*strippers*, ef kunvenient. My ole woman has burnt up, fust and last, nigh on to a hunded packs for me, and it's onpossible to keep 'em in the house. Thar's a new set of fellers come about, thinks they're smart at Poaker, which I want 'em to larn *me* a little. Never mind bout not sendin the money to pay for the dokkyments—I kin win the price of you when you come over, the first game, three up. Nothin more at present, only be purticler to keep that muscadine story back—and look here, Johns, quit ritin lies for the d—d feddul whigs, and come back to your ole prinsippels!"   Yours, in haist,

Simon Suggs.

Men of Tallapoosa, we have done! Suggs is before you! We have endeavoured to give the prominent events of his life with accuracy and impartiality. If you deem that he has " done the state some service," remember that he seeks the Sheriffalty of your county. He waxes old. He needs an office, the emoluments of which shall be sufficient to enable him to relax his intellectual exertions. His military services; his numerous family; his long residence among you; his gray hairs—all plead for him! Remember him at the polls!

TAKING THE CENSUS.

PART FIRST.

THE collection of statistical information concerning
the resources and industry of the country, by the assistant marshals who were employed to take the last
census, was a very difficult work. The popular impression, that a tremendous tax would soon follow the
minute investigation of the private affairs of the people, caused the census-taker to be viewed in no better
light than that of a tax-gatherer; and the consequence
was, that the information sought by him was either
withheld entirely, or given with great reluctance.
The returns, therefore, made by the marshals, exhibit
a very imperfect view of the wealth and industrial
progress of the country. In some portions of the
country the excitement against the unfortunate officers
—who were known as the "*chicken men*"—made it
almost dangerous for them to proceed with the business of taking the census; and bitter were the taunts,
threats, and abuse which they received on all hands,
but most particularly from the old women of the country. The dear old souls could not bear to be cate-
chised about the produce of their looms, poultry

149

yards, and dairies; and when they did "come down" upon the unfortunate inquisitor, it was with a force and volubility that were sure to leave an impression. We speak from experience, and feelingly, on this subject; for it so happened, that the Marshal of the Southern District of Alabama, "reposing especial confidence" in our ability, invested us one day with all the powers of assistant Marshal; and arming us with the proper quantity of blanks, sent us forth to count the noses of all the men, women, children, and chickens resident upon those nine hundred square miles of rough country which constitute the county of Tallapoosa. Glorious sport! thought we; but it didn't turn out so. True, we escaped without any drubbings, although we came unpleasantly near catching a dozen, and only escaped by a very peculiar knack we have of "sliding out;" but then we were quizzed, laughed at, abused, and nearly drowned. Children shouted "Yonder goes the chicken man!" Men said, "Yes, d—n him, he'll be after the *taxes* soon;—and the old women threatened, if he came to inquire about *their* chickens, "to set the dogs on him," while the young women observed "they didn't know what a man wanted to be so pertic'lar about gals' ages for, without he was a gwine a-courtin'." We have some reminiscences of our official peregrinations that will do to laugh at now, although the occurrences with which they are connected were, at the time, any thing but mirth inspiring to us.

We rode up one day to the residence of a widow rather past the prime of life—just that period at which nature supplies most abunda tly the oil which lubricates the hinges of the female tongue—and hitching to the fence, walked into the house.

"Good morning, madam," said we, in our usual bland, and somewhat insinuating manner.

"Mornin'," said the widow gruffly.

Drawing our blanks from their case, we proceeded —"I am the man, madam, that takes the census, and——"

"The mischief you are!" said the old termagant. "Yes, I've hearn of you; Parson W. told me you was coming, and I told him jist what I tell you, that if you said 'cloth,' 'soap,' *ur* 'chickens,' to *me*, I'd set the dogs on ye.—Here, Bull! here, Pomp!" Two wolfish curs responded to the call for Bull and Pomp, by coming to the door, smelling at our feet with a slight growl, and then laid down on the steps. "Now," continued the old she savage, "them's the severest dogs in this country. Last week Bill Stonecker's two year old steer jumped my yard fence, and Bull and Pomp tuk him by the throat, and they killed him afore my boys could break 'em loose, to save the world."

"Yes, ma'am," said we, meekly; "Bull and Pomp seem to be very fine dogs."

"You may well say that: what I tells them to do they do—and if I was to sick them on your old hoss yonder, they'd eat him up afore you could say Jack Roberson. And its jist what I shall do, if you try to pry into my consarns. They are none of your business, nor Van Buren's nuther, I reckon. Oh, old Van Banburen! I wish I had you here, you old rascal! *I'd* show you what—I'd—I'd make Bull and

Pomp show you how to be sendin' out men to take
down what little stuff people's got, jist to tax it, when
its taxed enough a'ready!"

All this time we were perspiring through fear of
the fierce guardians of the old widow's portal. At
length, when the widow paused, we remarked that
as she was determined not to answer questions about
the produce of the farm, we would just set down the
age, sex, and complexion of each member of her
family.

"No sich a thing—you'll do no sich a thing," said
she; "I've got five in family, and that's all you'll git
from me. Old Van Buren must have a heap to do,
the dratted old villyan, to send you to take down how
old my children is. I've got five in family, and they
are all between five and a hundred years old; they
are all a plaguy sight whiter than you, and whether
they are *he* or *she*, is none of your consarns."

We told her we would report her to the Marshal,
and she would be fined: but it only augmented her
wrath.

"Yes! send your marshal, or your Mr. Van Buren
here, if you're bad off to—let 'em come—let Mr. Van
Buren come"—looking as savage as a Bengal tigress
—"Oh, I wish he *would* come"—and her nostrils
dilated, and her eyes gleamed—"I'd cut his head
off!"

"That might kill him," we ventured to remark,
by way of a joke.

"Kill him! kill him—oh—if I had him here by the
years I reckon I *would* kill him. A pretty fellow to
be eating his vittils out'n gold spoons that poor

people's taxed for, and raisin' an army to get him made king of Ameriky—the oudacious, nasty, stinking old scamp!" She paused a moment, and then resumed, "And now, mister, jist put down what I tell you on that paper, and don't be telling no lies to send to Washington city. Jist put down 'Judy Tompkins, ageable woman, and four children.' "

We objected to making any such entry, but the old hag vowed it should be done, to prevent any misrepresentation of her case. We, however, were pretty resolute, until she appealed to the couchant whelps, Bull and Pomp. At the first glimpse of their teeth, our courage gave way, and we made the entry in a bold hand across a blank schedule—"Judy Tompkins, *ageable* woman and four children."

We now begged the old lady to dismiss her canine friends, that we might go out and depart: and forthwith mounting our old black, we determined to give the old soul a parting fire. Turning half round, in order to face her, we shouted—

" Old 'oman !"

" Who told you to call me old 'oman, you long-legged, hatchet-faced whelp, you? I'll make the dogs take you off that horse if you give me any more sarse. What do you want?"

" Do you want to get married ?"

" Not to you, if I do !"

" Placing our right thumb on the nasal extremity of our countenance, we said, "You needn't be uneasy, old 'un, on that score—thought you might suit sore-legged Dick S—— up our way, and should like to know what to tell him he might count on, if he come down next Sunday!"

"Here, Bull!" shouted the widow, "sick him, Pomp!" but we cantered off, unwounded, fortunately, by the fangs of Bull and Pomp, who kept up the chase as long as they could hear the cheering voice of their mistress—"Si-c-k, Pomp—sick, sick, si-c-k him, Bull—suboy! suboy! suboy!"

Our next adventure was decidedly a dangerous one. Fording the Tallapoosa river, where its bed is extremely uneven, being formed of masses of rock full of fissures, and covered with slimy green moss, when about two-thirds of the way across, we were hailed by Sol Todd from the bank we were approaching. We stopped to hear him more distinctly.

"Hellow! little 'squire, you a-chicken hunting to-day?"

Being answered affirmatively, he continued—"You better mind the holes in them ere rocks—if your horse's foot gits ketched in 'em you'll never git it out. You see that big black rock down to your right? Well, there's good bottom down below that. Strike down thar, outside that little riffle—and now cut right into that smooth water and come across!"

We followed Sol's directions to the letter, and plunging into the *smooth water*, we found it to be a basin surrounded with steep ledges of rock, and deep enough to swim the horse we rode. Round and round the poor old black toiled without finding any place at which he could effect a landing, so precipitous were the sides. Sol occasionally asked us "if the bottom was'nt first rate," but did nothing to help

us. At length we scrambled out, wet and chilled to
the bone—for it was a sharp September morning—
and continued our journey, not a little annoyed by the
boisterous, roaring laughter of the said Solomon, at
our picturesque appearance.

We hadn't more than got out of hearing of Sol's
cachinatory explosions, before we met one of his
neighbours, who gave us to understand that the duck-
ing we had just received, was but the fulfilment of a
threat of Sol's, to make the " chicken-man" take a
swim in the " Buck Hole " He had heard of our
stopping on the opposite side of the river the night
previous, and learning our intention to ford just where
we did, fixed himself on the bank to insure our finding the way into the " Buck Hole."

This information brought our nap right up, and re-
questing Bill Splawn to stay where he was till we returned, we galloped back to Sol's, and found that
worthy, rod on shoulder, ready to leave on a fishing
excursion.

" Sol, old fellow," said we, " that was a most unfortunate *lunge* I made into that hole in the river—
I've lost twenty-five dollars in specie out of my coat
pocket, and I'm certain it's in that hole, for I felt my
pocket *get light* while I was scuffling about in there.
The money was tied up tight in a buckskin pouch,
and I must get you to help me get it."

This of course, was a regular old-fashioned lie, as
we had not seen the amount of cash mentioned as lost,
in a " coon's age." It took, however, pretty well ;
and Sol concluded, as it was a pretty cold spell of
weather for the season, and the water was almost like

ice, that half the contents of the buckskin pouch
would be just about fair for recovering it. After
some chaffering, we agreed that Sol should dive for
the money "on shares," and we went down with
him to the river, to point out the precise spot at
which our pocket "grew light." We did so with
anxious exactness, and Sol soon denuded himself and
went under the water in the "Buck Hole," "like a
shuffler duck with his wing broke." Puff! puff! as
he rose to the surface. "Got it Sol!" ."No dang it,
hear goes again"—and Sol disappeared a second
time. Puff! puff! and a considerable rattle of teeth
as Sol once more rose into "upper air." "What
luck, old horse?" "By jings, I felt it that time, but
somehow it slid out of my fingers." Down went Sol
again, and up he came after the lapse of a minute,
still without the pouch. "Are you *right sure* 'squire,
that you lost it in this hole," said Sol, getting out upon
a large rock, while the chattering of his teeth divided
his words into rather more than their legitimate number of syllables. "Oh perfectly certain Sol, perfectly certain. You know twenty-five dollars in hard
money weigh a pound or two. I didn't mention the
circumstance when I first came out of the river, because I was so scared and confused that I didn't remember it—but I know just as well when the pouch
broke through my coat pocket, as can be!"

Thus reassured, Sol took the water again, and, as
we were in a hurry, we requested him to bring the
pouch and half the money to Dadeville, if his diving
should prove successful.

"To be sure I will," said he, and his blue lips

quivered with cold, and his whole frame shook from the same cause.

The " river ager" made Sol shake worse than that, that fall.

But we left him diving for the pouch industriously, and no doubt he would have got it, if it had been there!

Once, as we were about to leave a house at which we had put up the night previous, one of the girls—a buxom one of twenty—followed us to the fence, and the following *tete-a-tete* ensued:

" Now, 'squire they say you know, and I want you to tell me, *ef you please*—what *will* chickens be wuth this fall ?"

" How many have you ?"

" The rise of seventy, and three hens a-settin !"

" Well now, Miss Betsy," said we, " you know how much I set by the old man your daddy—and the old lady, you know how *she and me* always got along —and Jim and Dave, you know we was always like brothers—and yourself, Miss Betsy, I consider my particular friend—and as it's you, I'll tell you !"

" Do, 'squire, ef you please ; they say Van Buren's going to feed his big army on fowls ; and some folks say he's going to take 'em without payin' for 'em, and some say he aint—and I thought in course, ef he *did* pay for 'em, the price *would* rise !"

" Well, the fact is—but don't say nothing about it —the army *is* to be fed on fowls ; the *roosters* will be given to the officers to make 'em *brave*, and the hens to the common soldiers ; because, you see, they aint as good."

"In course!"

"So you see, the hens will be worth about three bits, and roosters a half a dollar, and ready sale, at that."

She was perfectly delighted, and we do not hesitate to say, would have rewarded us with a kiss, if we had asked it; but in those days modesty was the bright trait in our character. As it was, she only insisted on our taking "a bit of something cold" in our saddle-bags, in case we should reach town too late for dinner.

Our next encounter was with an old lady notorious in her neighbourhood for her garrulity and simple-mindedness. Her loquacity knew no bounds; it was constant, unremitting, interminable, and sometimes laughably silly. She was interested in quite a large chancery suit which had been " dragging its slow length along" for several years, and furnished her with a conversational fund which she drew upon extensively, under the idea that its merits could never be sufficiently discussed. Having been warned of her propensity, and being somewhat hurried when we called upon her, we were disposed to get through business as soon as possible, and without hearing her enumeration of the strong points of her law case. Striding into the house, and drawing our papers—

" Taking the census, ma'am!" quoth we.

"Ah! well! yes! bless your *soul*, honey, take a seat. Now do! Are you the gentleman that Mr. Van Buren has sent out to take the *sensis*? I wonder! well, good Lord look down, how *was* Mr. Van Buren and *family* when you seed him?"

We explained that we had never seen the president; didn't "know him from a side of sole leather;" and we had been written to, to take the census.

"Well, now, thar agin! Love your soul! Well, I 'spose Mr. Van Buren *writ* you a letter, did he? No? Well, I suppose some of his officers done it—bless my soul? Well, God be praised, there's mighty little *here* to take down—times is hard, God's will be done; but looks like people can't git their jest rights in this country; and the law is all for the rich and none for the poor, praise the Lord. Did you ever hear tell of that case my boys has got agin old Simpson? Looks like they never will git to the eend on it; glory to His name! The children will suffer I'm mightily *afeerd;* Lord give us grace. *Did* you ever see Judge B——? Yes? Well, the Lord preserve us! Did you ever here him say what he was agwine to do in the boys' case agin Simpson? No! Good Lord! Well, 'squire, *will* you ax him the next time you see him, and write me word; and tell him what I say; I'm nothing but a poor widow, and my boys has got no larnin, and old Simpson tuk 'em in. It's a mighty hard case on my boys any how. They ought to ha' had a mighty good start, all on 'em; but God bless you, that old man has used 'em up twell they aint able to buy a *creetur* to plough with. It's a mighty hard case, and the will oughtn't never to a been broke, but——"

Here we interposed and told the old lady that our time was precious—that we wished to take down the number of her family, and the produce raised by her

last year, and be off. After a good deal of trouble
we got through with the descriptions of the members
of her family, and the " statistical table" as far as the
article " cloth."

" How many yards of cotton cloth did you weave
in 1840, ma'am ?"

" Well, now! The Lord have mercy!—less see!
You know Sally Higgins that used to live down in
the Smith settlement ?—poor thing, her daddy *druv*
her off on the 'count of her havin' a little 'un, poor
creetur'—poor gal, she couldn't help it, I dare say.
Well, Sally she come to stay 'long wi' me when the
old man druv her away, and she was a powerful
good hand to weave, and I *did* think she'd help me
a power. Well, arter she'd bin here awhile, her
baby hit took sick, and old Miss Stringer she under-
tuk to help it—she's a powerful good hand, old Miss
Stringer, on roots, and yearbs, and sich like! Well,
the Lord look down from above! She made a sort
of a tea, as I was a-saying, and she gin it to Sally's
baby, but it got wuss—the poor creetur—and she gin
it tea, and gin it tea, and looked like, the more she
gin it tea, the more——"

" My dear madam, I am in a hurry—please tell
me how many yards of cotton cloth you wove in
1840. I want to get through with you and go on."

" Well, well, the Lord-a-mercy! who'd a thought
you'd 'a bin so snappish! Well, as I was a' sayin',
Sali's child hit kept a gittin' wuss, and old Miss
Stringer, she kept a givin' it the yearb tea twell at
last the child hit looked like hit *would* die any how.
And 'bout the time the child was at its wust, old

Daddy Sykes he come along, and he said if we'd git some night-shed berries, and stew 'em with a little cream and some hog's lard—now old daddy Sykes is a mighty fine old man, and he gin the boys a heap of mighty good counsel about that case—boys, says he, I'll tell you what you do; you go——"

"In God's name, old lady," said we, "tell about your cloth, and let the sick child and Miss Stringer, Daddy Sykes, the boys, and the law suit go to the devil. I'm in a hurry!"

"Gracious bless your dear soul! don't git aggra-wated. I was jist a tellin' ycu how it come I didn't weave no cloth last year."

"Oh, well, you didn't weave *any* cloth last year. Good! we'll go on to the next article."

"Yes! you see the child hit begun to swell and turn *yaller*, and hit kept a *wallin'* its eyes and a moanin', and I knowed——"

"Never mind about the child—just tell me the value of the poultry you raised last year."

"Oh, well—yes—the chickens you mean. Why, the Lord love your poor soul, I reckon you never in your *born* days seen a poor creefur have the luck that I did—and looks like we never shall have good luck agin; for ever sence old Simpson tuk that case up to the chancery court——"

"Never mind the case; let's hear about the chick-ens, if you please."

"God bless you, honey, the *owls* destroyed *in and about* the best half what I did raise. Every blessed night the Lord sent, they'd come and set on the comb

of the house, and *hoo-hoo hoo*, and one night partick-
lar, I remember, I had jist got up to the night-shed
salve to '*nint* the little gal with ——"

" Well, well, what was the value of what you did
raise ?"

" The Lord above look down!   They got so bad
—the owls did—that they tuk the *old hens*, as well's
the young chickens.   The night I was telling 'bout,
I hearn somethin' *squall! squall!* and says, I'll bet
that's old Speck that nasty oudacious owl's got ; for I
seen her go to roost with her chickens, up in the
plum tree, *fornenst* the smoke house.   So I went to
whar old Miss Stringer was sleepin'. and says I, *Miss*
Stringer!   *Oh!* Miss *Stringer!* sure's you're born,
that stinkin' owl's got old Speck out'n the plum tree ;
weil, old Miss Stringer she turned over 'pon her side
like, and says she, what did you say, Miss Stokes?
and says I——"

We began to get very tired, and signified the same
to the old lady, and begged she would answer us directly, and without any circumlocution.

" The Lord Almighty love your dear heart, honey,
I'm tellin' you as fast as I kin.   The owls they got
worse *and* worse, after they'd swept old Speck and
all *her* gang, they went to work on 'tothers ; and
Bryant (that's one of my boys,) he 'lowed he shoot
the pestersome creeturs—and so one night arter that,
we hearn one holler, and Bryant, he tuk the old mus-
ket and went out, and sure enough, there was *owley*,
(*as he thought*,) a-settin' on the comb of the house ;
so he blazed away and down come —— what on

airth did come down, do you reckon; when Bryant fired?"

" The owl, I suppose."

" No sich a thing, no sich! the owl *warn't thar.* 'Twas my old house-cat come a tumblin' down, spittin', sputterin', and scratchin', and the furr a flyin' every time she jumped, like you'd a busted a feather bed open! Bryant he said, the way he come to shoot the cat instead of the owl, he seed something white——"

" For Heaven's sake Mrs. Stokes, give me the value of your poultry, or *say you will not!* Do one thing or the other."

" Oh, well, dear love your heart, I reckon I had last year nigh about the same as I've got this."

" Then tell me how many dollars worth you have now, and the thing's settled."

" I'll let you see for yourself," said the widow Stokes, and taking an ear of corn out of a crack between the logs of the cabin, and shelling off a handful, she commenced scattering the grain, all the while screaming, or rather *screeching*—" chick—chick—chick—chick-ee—chick-ee—chick-ee—ee!"

Here they came, roosters, and hens, and pullets, and little chicks—crowing, cackling, chirping; flying and fluttering over beds, chairs, and tables; alighting on the old woman's head and shoulders, fluttering against her sides, pecking at her hands, and creating a din and confusion altogether indescribable. The old lady seemed delighted, thus to exhibit her feathered " stock," and would occasionally exclaim—"a nice *passel*, aint they—a nice passel!"   But she never would say what they were worth; no persuasion could bring her to the point; and our papers at Washington contain no estimate of the value of the widow Stokes' poultry, though, as she said her herself, she had "*a mighty nice passel!*"

"HII RUNCKER," FIDLER BILL, AND THE DOG, "JIM"

PART SECOND.

WHEN we were taking the census in Tallapoosa, we had a rare frolic at old Kit Kuncker's, up on Union creek, which we must tell about. But first let us introduce uncle Kit.

Old Kit was a fine specimen of the old-fashioned Georgia wagoner, of the glorious old times when locomotives didn't whiz about in every direction. He was brought up on the road, and retained a fondness for his early vocation, though now in comparative affluence. Uncle Kit was sixty years old, we suppose, but the merriest old dog alive; and his chirrupping laugh sounded every minute in the day. Particularly fond of female society, his great delight was to plague the "womanhood" of his household and settlement, in every possible way. His waggery, of one sort or other, was incessant; and as he was the patriarch of his neighbourhood—having transplanted every family in it, with himself, from Georgia—his jokes were all considered good jokes, and few dared be offended at his good-humored satire. Besides all this, Uncle Kit was a devoted Jackson man, and an inveterate hater of all nullifiers: hence the name of his creek.

Two "chattels" had Mr. Kuncker which he prized beyond all his other possessions—one of these was a big yellow dog that followed the wagon, and among other accomplishments, predicted the future. Uncle Kit called him Andy, in honor of General Jackson.

The other favourite was a fine old roan horse, named
" Fiddler Bill," upon which, when a little " drinky,"
he was wont to exhibit very fair horsemanship in the
streets, or rather, the street of Dudleyville.

We were making an entry of somebody's chickens
at a store door in the village just mentioned, one Au-
gust day, when a familiar " hillo !" reached our ear,
and turning round, we perceived, some twenty yards
off, the quizzical face of our old friend, projecting
over the fore-gate of his wagon, and puckered into
five hundred little wrinkles as he cachinnated joy-
ously—

" Hillo, 'squire! bless your little *union* snake-skin,
yer uncle Kit's *so* glad to see you, ha! ha! I'm jist
back from Wetumpky, he! he! ya! You see, yer
uncle Kit's been down to git the trimmins for neice
Susy's weddin, next Thursday night. You must
come over 'squire—it's Jim Spraggins that's gwine
to pick up Suse; you see yer uncle Kit waited for you
twell he found you *wouldn't* talk it out, he! he! ha!
—come over, as *I* was a-sayin, and you kin take the
sensis of the whoʹe krick at one settin, and buss all
the gals besides, he! a! yah! yah!

We thanked uncle Kit, and told him we would
come; wheʹ ʹupon the jovial old fellow whistled to
Andy—who had stepped into the " grocery," thinking that, of course, his master would stop *there*, any
how—" clucked" to Fiddler Bill, who worked in the
lead, cracked the steers at the wheels, and so started.

In a moment we heard the sharp " hillo !" again.

" You must be sure to come, 'squire," said uncle
Kit, stopping his team so as to be heard ; " yer aunt

Hetty will look for you certain, he! he!—and if she can raise somethin for you to eat, and a year or two o' corn for your horse, *any way in the world*, you will be as welcome to it as the water that runs;" and Mr. Kuncker chuckled terribly at the bare idea of our aunt Hetty's being straitened to provide viands for animals human or equine!

We repeated our assurances that we should attend; and uncle Kit reassuming the lines, said—"Well, *now* I'm off sure, 'squire! God bless you and Gin- nel Jackson, and d—n the nullifiers! Wake up, Fid! Good bye"—and rolled off.

Once again, however, he stopped and shouted back—"Don't be a   d to come! Yer uncle Kit has fust-rate *spring-u ɛ er*, allers on hand!" and he chuckled longer than before, at the wit of calling *corn-whiskey* "spring-water;" and put his finger by the side of his old cut-water of a nose! So lively an old dog was uncle Kit Kuncker!

On the appointed evening, we arrived at Mr. Kuncker's about dark. The old man was waiting at the fence to receive us.

"Bless your *union* soul, little squire," he said, shaking our extended hand with both of his; "yer uncle Kit is as proud to see you, as ef he'd a found a silver dollar with a hole through it! Hetty!" he shouted, "here's the God-blessed little union 'squire come to see his uncle! Come out and see him, he! he! yah! and, mind and throw a meal-bag, or some- thin else over your head, twell my little 'squire gits sorter usen to the *big ugly!* Make haste you old dried-up witch! Ef you can't find the bag, take yer apern! he! he! e! a! yah!" and uncle Kit laughed till he cried.

Mrs. Kuncker presently made her appearance—not with the meal-bag over her head, however—and greeted us most hospitably.

"Don't mind old Kit's romancin 'squire," she observed; "I'm afeard he'll be a fool all his days. We've been married now, gwine on forty year, and he's never spoke the fust sensible word yit!"

"Sorter shade your eyes, long at fust, 'squire," remarked uncle Kit, as he busied himself in "stripping" our steed, "when you look at yer aunt Hetty. The *ugly's* out on her wuss nor the small-pox! ha! ha! yah! and I'm bound to keep it out too, wi' all sorts o' warm teas. The Lord will be mighty apt to call her home ef ever it strikes in 'm a-thinkin"—and uncle Kit laughed again, while he placed our saddle upon the fence, with twenty others.

"Come in, 'squire," said aunt Hetty, "or that poor light-headed old critter 'ill laugh hisself to death!" and we walked with her into Mr. Kuncker's neat, *framed* dwelling—the only building of the sort on Union creek.

The big room of uncle Kit's house was full of light and of company. Most of the latter were known to us, but there were some strange faces; and with these we determined to get acquainted as soon as possible. A little removed from the bustling part of the congregation, we observed a fat woman, of middle age, with a sleepy expression of face. A little way from her feet, and sprawling on the floor, was a chubby child, about eighteen months old, whose little coat was pinned up, by the hem behind, to its collar; thus leaving no inconsiderable portion of its person exposed. "He e," thought we," is an interesting family: let's take it down;" and approaching the dame, we drew our papers, having first saluted her.

"Gracious! stranger!" she ejaculated, "what're you arter?"

"Only taking the census."

"Sally! oh, Sally Hetson! *do* run here," said Mrs. Naron—for that proved to be her name—"ef here aint the man we've hearn so much 'bout! Here's the *chicken-man!* I do wonder!" she continued, surveying us from crown to sole; "Well! hit's the *slimmest* critter, to be sure, ever *I* seed; Hit's legs, I *do* declar, is not as big as my Thomas Jefferson's! Come here Thomas Jefferson, and let manne thee ef your legth aint ath big ath hitthen!" addressing the youngster on the floor.

But Thomas Jefferson did not heed the invitation, but continued to dabble and splash in a little pool of water, which had somehow got there, as proud, apparently, of his *sans-culottism*, as ever his illustrious name-sake could have been of his.

"Don't you *hear* me, Thomas Jefferson?" screamed the mother—"don't you hear me, you little torment?"

Thomas Jefferson *did* hear this time, and hastened to obey. He raised himself up, spread out his fat arms to preserve his equilibrium, turned half round, lost it, and was instantly seated in the miniature pool, with a splash that sent several droplets into his mother's face.

Mrs. Naron flew at the child with an energy that contrasted strongly with her oleaginous appearance; and seizing him by the middle, held him up *inverted*, with one hand, while with the other she inflicted what, in our nursery days, would have been called a "sound spanking"—which finished, she reseated herself, and brought him down in a sitting position upon her knee, with sufficient violence to produce a sudden abbreviation of as dreadful a howl as ever vexed human ear.

We didn't altogether relish these indications of a vivacious temperament in Mrs. Naron, and accordingly made our examination as short and smooth as possible. And when she demurred to furnishing the statistical information, because she "never *had* done sich a thing afore," we admitted the cogency of the reason, and pressed the matter no further; for we were convinced that the government did not expect its officers to run the risk of what Master Thomas Jefferson Naron had got, merely to add another dozen yards of cloth, or score of chickens, to the estimated wealth of the country!

There was now a slight bustle in one corner, for which, at first, we couldn't account. It was among a group of young persons, male and female, who appeared to be urging one of their number to do something which he was unwilling, or affected to be unwilling to do. "Do now Pete!" "Oh you *kin*—you *know* you kin!" "Pshaw! I wouldn't be a fool!" "Jist this *one* time, Pete!" were some of the exclamations and expostulations that we heard. They were not without effect: a young man in a blue-coat,

Mrs. Varon flew at the child with an energy that contrasted strongly with
her oleaginous appearance and seizing him by the middle,
held him up *inverted* with one hand

with big brass buttons, cleared his throat, and commenced singing to a tune whiningly dolorous, nasal,
unvaried, and interminable, the popular ditty of

"THE OLD BACHELARE."

Come, *while* you set silent, I'll have you to hear,
The truth or a lie, from an old bachela*r e:*
They'll set and they'll think, twell they war out their brains,
And wish for a wife—but it is all in vain—
    Sing down, dary down."

Before this verse was half-finished, Andy, (the
dog,) who was coiled up in the entry, commenced a
howling accompaniment, worse even, than the vocal-
ism of Mr. Peter Marks, who looked vexed and confused, and stopped singing.

"I wouldn't mind it, Peter," said good old Mrs.
Kuncker, who now approached; "I wouldn't mind it.
Its nothin but that dratted yaller brute of old Kit's;
and, bless the Lord, its *jist* the way he does *me*, constant—his master's larnt it to him—I never kin begin
to sing, 'I rode on the sky, quite ondestified I,' or
'Primrose,' or 'Zion,' or *any* of them sperechal
himes, but what the stinkin, yaller cuss strikes up his
everlastin howl, and jist makes me quit whether or
no!" and aunt Hetty went and drove Andy away!

"He! he! yah! yah! e-e- yah!" chuckled uncle
Kit—" aint Andy got a noble v'ice? *Aint* he, squire?
yah! yah! *He* sings *bass,* and yer aunt Hetty sings
tribble, and I'm gwine to git a middlin-size dog to
sing *tenor,* and then we'll be fixed—he! he! yah!—
and you must come over every other Sunday to yer
uncle Kit's singing school!"—laughing immoderately
at the conceit.

And Hetty said "pish!" with a worried air, and Mr. Marks re-tuned his pipes:

> But when you are married, it is for to please,
> And when you have children you're never at ease;
> You'll go bare and stint, just to make 'em suppo't,
> But a bachelor's care is his back and his throat,
>   Sing down, dary down!"

The applause being loud and enthusiastic, Mr. Marks passed his right hand over his well-tallowed side locks, glanced at the buttons of his coat, cleared his throat, and proceeded to give the other side of the picture:

> "But when you are gone, your wife will prepar',
> A dish of fine dainties, or somethin' that's rar',
> So smilin' and pleasin' when you do draw near—
> There's no such delight for the old bache*lare!*
>   Sing down, dary down.

Andy, by this time, had got under the house, and accompanied the singer in the two last lines and the chorus, without any particular reference to "time," but with an earnestness that showed that the love of music was in his soul. Mr Marks bit his lips and frowned, but as he had only one more verse to sing, determined to try and get through with it:

> "When *I* go abroad, and sich things I do see—"

(Andy howled furiously.)

> "I wish, but in vain, that it only was me"—

("Oo–oo–au–e–au–oo–oo–oo!" from the dog!)

> "Whilst *I* must both breeches and petticoat ware"—

(Andy kept " *even along.*")

> "It grieves me to think I'm an old bache*lare,*
>   Sing down, dary down "

Andy howled through the last line beautifully, but getting into the chorus, commenced a series of barks which seemed likely to be prolonged indefinitely.

"My poor dog!" exclaimed Mr. Kuncker, affecting great anxiety, "my poor dog has got *tangled up* in that *cussed* tune, and 'ill choke hisself to death! Run Jim,"—to his son—"and ontie the blasted thing, or cut it in two! yah e–e yah! yah! yaw!"

"Bein as my kumpny aint adceptable *here*, I'll dismiss," said Mr. Marks, the vocalist, in a pet; at the same time buttoning up his blue swallow-tail, and sleeking down his greasy locks.

"Couldn't you give us somethin *sperechal* before you go?" asked uncle Kit, "your aunt Hetty and Andy's tip-top on *sperechal* songs;" and the wrinkles on Mr. Kuncker's face formed themselves into fifty little smilets.

"Kee–yow! yow!" all of a sudden from Andy, as he run from under the house.

"Make up your bread with *that!*" said aunt Hetty, as she raised up with the tea-kettle in her hand, from which she had been pouring boiling water through a crack upon Andy.

"Old 'oman!" said uncle Kit passionately, "I'll take that dog kleen away"—thinking, in the energy of his own affection for Andy, that the announcement would have a decidedly painful effect upon the mind of his wife—"and you never shall set eyes upon him agin, *as long as you live!*"

"I—only—wish—to—the—Lord—in—heaven— you *would!*" said aunt Hetty, emphatically shaking her head between each word.

" I won't do no sich a thing!" said old Kit, in the
spirit of contradiction ; "'I'll keep him here *allers*, jist
to sing!   He shall sing ' Primrose' "—

" Can't help it!"

" And ' Zion,' and—"

" Can't help that nuther!"

" ' Won't you come and go with me,' and—"

" Don't care!"

" And all the rest of the songs in the Mezooree
Harmony, and ' Mearcer's Cluster,' too!   Cust ef he
shan't!"

" Well! well! Christoper, old man!" said aunt
Hetty, in a conciliatory tone; " don't be aggrawated.
I oughtent to fret you I know ; and ef Andy'll behave
hisself like a decent dog—like Bull Wilkerson, now,
for a sample, which never comes in the hou—"

" Thar aint"—said uncle Kit, swelling with indignation at the indirect attack upon the morals of his
dog—" thar aint a dog of a better karackter in the
settlement than Andy Kuncker—Bull Wilkerson or
no Bull Wilkerson!   No! thar aint no better, nor no
gentlemanlier a dog in the *whole county*, than Andy!
Savin the presence of this kumpny, I'll be *damned* ef
thar is!" and having so spoken, Mr. Kuncker went
out to seek his dog and console him in his afflictions.

As soon as Mr. Kuncker returned, the couple desirous of matrimony, took the floor, and 'squire Berry
united them in the bonds of wedlock, after the most
summary fashion.   Uncle Kit then announced that
some " cold scraps" were to be found in an adjoining
room—which said " cold scraps" consisted, princi-
pally, of one or two half-grown hogs baked brown ;

two or three very fat turkeys; a hind quarter of beef;
together with about a half wagon-load of bread, cake,
pies, stewed fruit, and so forth.

"'Squire! 'squire! don't set *thar!*" said uncle Kit,
addressing himself to us, as we were taking a chair
among the masculine portion of the guests; "oh, no!
he! yah! yah! your uncle Kit didn't bring you here
for that, yah! yah! yah! Here's a little gal has never
had her *sensis* taken, and I want you to see ef you
kan't git 'em, yah! yah!" and uncle Kit forced us
into a chair, greatly against our will, by the side of
Miss Winny Folsom, a very pretty girl, with a pout-
ing mouth. Mr. Kuncker drew up a chair behind us.

Standing near uncle Kit's back, we observed a
young man who, somehow or other, took a great ap-
parent interest in either Miss Winny or ourself; but
he said nothing. He was a rare specimen of the
piney-woods species of the genus homo. His face
was not unhandsome, but he had a considerable
stoop of the shoulders, and was knock-kneed to
deformity. His coat was "blue mixed," with a
very acute terminus, and it seemed to have a
particular affection for the hump of his shoulders,
for it touched no other part of his person. His pantaloons were of buff cassimere—most probably bought
at second-hand—and contracted, from excessive
washing, or some other cause, to a painful scantiness.
There was a *white* "streak" between his vest and the
waistband, and a *red* one between the ends of the
legs and the tops of his white cotton socks. A pair
of red-leather straps, some twenty inches long, exerted
themselves to keep the legs down to this mark; but

every time that Mr. Isaac Hetson—that was his name —stooped, the pantaloons had slightly the advantage, by reason of the superior elasticity of the straps, and the *red* streak was, on every such occasion, made a little wider.

"Talk to her, 'squire! talk to her!" said uncle Kit; "when yer uncle Kit was young, he did'nt do nothin but talk to the gals, he—e—yah! yah!"

We endeavoured to make ourself agreeable to Miss Winny of course, and during the whispering of one of those confidential nothings common in such circumstances, our head came almost in contact with hers.   Seizing the opportunity, Mr. Kuncker brought *his* close up, and with his lips produced such an explosion as might have resulted, had we kissed Miss Winny.

"Ha!" exclaimed the old fellow, starting back in well-feigned amazement; "at it a'ready, 'squire! Well! 'twas a *buster*, any way!"—whereupon he laughed immoderately, as did most of the company. Miss Winny turned red, and *we* looked foolish—we suppose.

"Some people's too derned smart, any how!" said the gentleman in buff cassimere, who supposed that we had really kissed Miss Winny.

"And some aint smart enough, Ikey Hetson," said uncle Kit; "or they wouldn't let other people cut 'em out—would they Winny?"

Winny smiled, but said nothing, and Mr. Kuncker raising himself half up, so as again to intercept Mr. Hetson's view, produced another explosion.

"For shame, 'squire!" said he, sitting down again.

"I kin whip any pocket-knife lawyer that ever made a moccasin track in Dates*ville*" said Ike, striding backward and forward behind Mr. Kuncker's chair, like a lion in his cage—furiously jealous.

Uncle Kit laughed until his wife called to him across the room, and told him he was "a stark naitral old fool!"

"I wouldn't be a gump, ef I was you, Ike Hetson," remarked Miss Winny.

"Them that don't care nothin for me," replied Ike, "I don't care nothin for them, nuther."

"The 'squire's mouth aint *pisen*, I reckon," said Miss Winny, very sharply; "and it wouldn't *kill* a body ef he *did* kiss 'em!"

"Let's see!" said we, doing *that same* before Miss Winny could help herself.

"Go it! my rip-roarin, little union 'squire: you're elected!" shouted uncle Kit, in a paroxysm of delight.

"Dern my everlastin dog-skin ef I'll stand it!" said the furious lover—"I'll die in my tracks fust! I'm jist as good as town folks, ef they *do* war shoe-boots and store close. I'm jist a hunderd and forty sev*ing* pound, *neat* weight, and I'm a wheel-horse!" and then Mr. Hetson doubled his fists and shook himself all over, with an energy that looked dangerous, considered in reference to the excessive tightness of his buff cassimeres.

Aunt Hetty now interposed—"Do Ikey! do now, son, *don't* be fretted so—*don't* be so jealous-hearted! The 'squire didn't mean *no* harm *in* the world, by

P

bussin Winny; and Winny didn't mean none by lettin of him—"

"I didn't let him: he done it hisself!" said Winny very quickly—and then she pouted.

"Oh, well! we all know *that*, to be sure," said aunt Hetty. "It were jist the romancin of that simple old crittur, that's never easy without he's got somebody in a brile. I wouldn't mind it, Ikey, no more'n I would—"

But Mr. Hetson *did* mind it; and he didn't wait for aunt Hetty to fish up a figure whereby to illustrate its insignificance, before he made a "burst" at us—but Mr. Kuncker caught him by the shoulder.

"Stop!" said uncle Kit

"*What?*" inquired Hetson.

Uncle Kit paused, and then slowly, but most emphatically remarked:

"*You'll—tar—them—trowsers!*"—and the whole company laughed at uncle Kit's remark, or Ike Hetson's trowsers—or perhaps, at both. And Ike hung down his head, and was evidently "used up."

"Thar's but *one* way to settle this, and to know who's to have Winny—you, or my little union 'squire."

"How's that?" asked Hetson.

"*Andy* will tell us all about it!"

Mr. Hetson turned very pale, for he had great faith in the predictions of Andy.

A general rush—supper being over—to the big room, followed this announcement, and uncle Kit whistled Andy into the house. The dog-prophet came in slowly and crouchingly, for the fear of his

mistress was before his eyes; and as he got opposite
Mrs. Kuncker, he emitted a deprecatory whine, and
with a bound attained his master's legs. Aunt Hetty,
however, made no attempt to strike him.

"Now, Andy, boy," said uncle Kit, "I've fetched
you in here, to tell all about Miss Winny Folsom's
fortin; and you must do it mighty nice and good, for
she's a pretty little *union* gal!" He then set about
drawing a huge circle, and several smaller circles
within, and an immense number of *radii;* and between these, rude representations of animals, both
real and fabulous—while Andy sat by, wagging his
tail, and looking very intelligent.

"It *a–i–n–t* right—it *a–i–n–t* right!—it's *a–g–i–n*
Scriptur'!" said granny Whipple, shaking her head,
and dwelling on the italicised words, as she surveyed
the necromantic operations of old Kit—"you're a-
doin of a *w–r–o–n–g* thing, Christopher Kuncker! I
t–e–ll you you are!" But Mr. Kuncker only laughed
at granny Whipple.

While Mr. Kuncker was engaged in preparing for
the delivery of the oracles, secundum artem, the conversation in the room turned on the degree of credit
to be given them.

"What do you think 'bout Andy's fortin tellin,
Miss Wilkerson?" asked Mrs. Naron. "*Do* you
believe he *raaly* knows what's gwine to come to
pass?"

"Well, now," replied Mrs. Wilkerson, I don't
know what *tu* say. It's a mighty strange thing how
knowin some brutes is. Thar's my "Cherry" cow,
I raaly b'lieve the critter knows when I'm a-gwine to

feed her *jist* as well as I do my own *dear* self! That minute I picks up my tub to go and tote her the slops, she'll ' moo,' and ' moo,' *and* ' moo.' And the know-inest look out of her eyes you ever seen a critter have in all your days!'"

" Oh law !" exclaimed several old women.

" Miss Kuncker, what do *you* say to it ?"—queried the first speaker—" you *oughter* know, ef any body does. He's *your* old man's dog. *Does* Andy know the futur, or not ?"

" It's a mighty hard thing," said aunt Hetty, " a *mighty* hard thing to spend a 'pinion 'pon. Some-times I think it's only Kit's devilment—and then agin, the dog *do* tell sich quar things, looks like I'm *'bleeged* to think he knows. Last week, I b'lieve it was—yes, *only* last week—Jim Hissup fotch a two gallon jug o' sperrets home, for the old man, from town. Well! Kit he 'spicioned Jim o' drinkin some on the way, but Jim denied it mighty bitter. So the old man fotch Andy in the house, and Andy give the sign that Jim *had* tuk some ! and then Jim right away *owned to it*, and told the old man *how much* he tuk, which was two drinks, as nigh as I can re-member !'"

" Good gracious !" burst from three or four.

" *I* don't believe nothin about it," said a withered old crone, as she sucked away industriously to pre-vent her pipe going out; " I *know* Andy can tell what'll happen. Brutes, in a common way," she continued aphoristically, as she pushed down the to-bacco in the bowl of her pipe with her fore-finger—

"is more knowiner 'an humans. Did y° ever hear, 'mongst ye, of the snake at John Green's?"

"Dear Saviour alive!" exclaimed a dozen—"what about the snake?" and they all drew long breaths and opened their eyes at one another.

"I'll tell ye! John Green's sister, (the grass widder, as lives with 'em,) she goes to her battlin bench, and what does she see thar, a-quiled up on it, a-sunnin of itself, but a big black snake—"

"Laws a-massey!" ejaculated the entire group.

"Jest as I tells ye—*thar it was!* and it licked out its tongue—it *did*, as sure's you're born—*right* at the widder, and looked the venomousest ever was! Well, she run in the house and fainted right away; and ef you'll b'lieve *me*, the very *next* week, her little boy, as can jest run about, *swallowed a punkin seed*, and like to a' died. Ef its uncle hadn't a' hit it on the back and a' made the punkin seed fly out, that child *never* would a' drawd another breath no more'n—shah! you may tell *me* that snakes and dogs don't know things, but"—and granny Richards didn't finish the sentence, but bobbed her head emphatically, as much as to say that *she* couldn't be humbugged by any such assertions.

Every thing was now ready: the rings, the radii, the serpents, the bats, the unicorns, and the scorpions, all complete; and Andy was seen seated in the exact centre of the whole, upon his hind legs, and looking very wise.

"Yes!" said uncle Kit, mentally contrasting Andy with Mrs. Kuncker's favourite; "Bull Wilkerson would look *devlish* well, settin thar on *his* hind legs!

Bull Wilkerson! *He aint got the power about him!*"
Then explaining to the company that Andy would
throw off the cheese without attempting to catch it, if
he wished to express a negative; but would toss it
up and receive it in his jaws, should he intend to
speak affirmatively—he placed a slice of home-made
cheese upon the dog's nose.

The company stood around, but outside of the
largest circle, Ike Hetson's protruding head thrust
farther towards Andy and old Kit, than any body
else's.   His face was anxious and cadaverous, but
he strove to suppress his feelings.

"Now Andy," began uncle Kit; "look at your
old master.   "Horum-scorum—ef—Mister—Ikey—
Hetson — is — to— be—married—to—Miss—Winny
—Folsom—say so!""

Andy threw the cheese on the floor, and thereupon
several old women screamed; and the Adam's apple
of Mr. Hetson's neck became a very large pippin, in
his attempt to swallow his grief.   "I *knowd* it!"
said he, in tones the most dolorous, while the corners
of his mouth twitched involuntarily and spasmo-
dically.

"Now Andy," said old Kit, replacing the cheese
on Andy's nose : "Horum-scorum—ef—my—little—
blessed—union— 'squire—is—a-gwine—to—get—
Miss Winny—say so *quick!*

Up went the cheese, and down again it came, into
Andy's sepulchral throat!

"Damn the varmint!"" ejaculated Mr. Hetson, and
bursting into the magic circle, he kicked Andy ve-
hemently in the side.

'Now Andy' said old Kit, replacing the cheese on Andy's nose'

"Fair fight! nobody tech!—sick him Andy!" shouted uncle Kit, in a rage at the breach of the peace committed on the person of his dog.

Andy dashed gallantly at Mr. Hetson, and seizing one of his red-leather straps, tore it on one side from the buff cassimere, which, frightened from "its propriety" by the display of canine teeth, retreated, instanter, to the neighbourhood of Mr. Hetson's knee! In his struggle to get away from the dog, Ike fell backwards over Master Thomas Jefferson Naron; and as his bare and unstrapped leg flew up, nearly at right angles with his body—while its fellow, held quiet by leather and cassimere, lay rigid along the floor—an uproarious shout of laughter at the grotesque spectacle shook the whole house.

"Well!" said the poor fellow as he got up on his *freed* leg—the other wouldn't work—"the jig's up now—'taint no use to make a fuss about it—but I wouldn't mind it so bad, ef 'twarn't that *he* was to git her. Anyhow, I'm off for the Arkansaw!—good by, Winny!" And off he did go, in spite of old Mrs. Kuncker's most strenuous efforts to detain him, and convince him that "Andy didn't know a thing about it, no more'n the man in the moon!"

As for Winny—the little fool!—she wept bitterly, as if there were no straight-legged men that would have been glad to marry her!

*   *   *   *   *   *

"'Squire," said old Kit, as he lighted us to bed, "you've not taken many *sensis* to-night?"

"Only one or two."

"Well, it's yer uncle Kit's fault! He *will* have

his fun, yah' yah' and Ike Hetson's e–e–yah–yah!
Never mind; come over next week, and yer uncle
Kit will go all through the settle*ment* wi' you, and
down on the river, and to Jim Kent's, which has got
a sister so ugly the flies won't light on her face—wuss
nor yer aunt Hetty, yah' yah'   And yer uncle Kit
will tell you how he and his Jim fooled the man from
the big-norrod outen Fiddler Bill, as we go 'long;
and Becky Kent will tell you 'bout the frolic me and
her had in the krick, the time she started to mill and
didn't git thar, yah, yah, e–e–e–yah!"

" Very well, uncle Kit; sure to come!"

" And 'squire, ef you want one o' Andy's puppies,
let yer uncle Kit know, and he'll save you a raal
peart one, eh?   Good night!   God bless the old
Ginnul, and damn all nullifiers!

DADDY BIGGS' SCRAPE

AT COCKERELL'S BEND.

COCKERELL'S BEND is a well-known rendezvous for the hunter and fisher of the Tallapoosa; and a beautiful place it is. The upper end of the curve is lake-like in its stillness, and is very deep; while a half mile below the river spreads itself to double its usual width, and brawls among rocks and islets fringed with the tall river grass. The part above is resorted to by those who fish with the rod; and that below, by seiners. Opposite the deep water, the hills come towering down to within twenty yards of the river, the narrow intervening strip being low land, covered with a tremendous growth of gum, poplar, and white-oak. Late in the afternoon of a warm May day, this part of the Bend is a most delightful spot. The little mountains on the south and west exclude the sun-glare completely, and the mere comfort-seeker may lay himself flat in the bottom of the old Indian canoe he finds moored there by a grape vine, and float and look at the clouds, and dream—as I have often done —with no living thing in sight to disturb his meditations, except the muskrat on the end of the old projecting log, and the matronly summer duck with her

189

brood of tiny ducklings, swimming, close huddled, in
the shadow of the huge wateroak, whose overhanging limbs are covered with a close net-work of muscadine vines—whereof, (of the vines I mean,) I have
a story of my friend Captain Suggs, which will be
related at the proper time. Take care! ye little downy
rascals!—especially you, little fellow, with half an
egg-shell stuck to your back!—true, there are not
many or large rout in the Tallapoosa: but there are
some, and occasionally one is found of mouth sufficient to engorge a young duck!—and almost always
in a cool quiet shade just like——hist! snap!—there
you go, precisely as I told you!   Now, old lady, quit
that fussing and fluttering, and take the "young
'uns" out of the way of that *other one* that isn't far
off!   Trituration in a trout's maw *must* be unpleasant one would think!

The "Bend" took its name from one Bob Cockerell, who, some years ago, inhabited a log hut on the
north side, within halloo of the river. Bob, by the
bye, was an equivocal sort of fellow—*people* said he
subsisted on stolen beef!—he challenged them, always, to "perduce the years;" and swore that he
lived honestly, by fishing. Be this as it may, it is
certain that his daughters, Betsy and Margaret, were
the naiads of the Bend; and all the " old settlers"
thereabouts have, at one time or another, been indebted to them for a passage across. They were not,
we may well suppose, as graceful or romantic as the
Lady of the Lake; but "Mag," with her blue eyes,
flowing hair, and " cutty sark"-—arranged with special
reference to the average depth of water in the bottom

of the canoe—was, at least, as pretty. And "the best day" the Scotch woman "ever saw," I'd venture the little Tallapoosian could have beaten her, easily, in a "single dash of a mile," with the paddles! They are gone now! but wherever they are, bless them!—they never kept one waiting as some male ferry-keepers do, but were aye at the "landing," and in the boat, before the echo of your shout had crossed the river!

It chanced once, that the writer encamped for a day or two on the narrow strip spoken of, with a company of the unsophisticated dwellers of the rough lands in that region, of whom the principal personage was " DADDY ELIAS BIGGS," sometimes called " DADDY 'LIAS," but more commonly, " *Daddy Biggs*." We were on a fishing expedition, and at night hung a short line or two from the branches of the trees which oversweep the water there, for "cat." One night, as we had just done this, and were gathered around the fire, a gallon jug passing from hand to hand, " Daddy Biggs"—who was a short, squab man, rosy-cheeked, bald, and "inclining to three-score"— remarked, as he extended his hand towards a long, gaunt fellow, with a very long nose, and a very black beard—

" Boys, ain't you never hearn what a h–ll of a scrape I had here, at this very spot, last year? Billy Teal, let me have a suck at that yeathen-war, and I'll tell you all about it."

The old man tuk " a suck," smacked his lips, and began his relation:

" You all 'member the time, boys, when them Cha-

tohospa fellows come here a fishin'?   D—n 'em, I
wish they could fish about home, without goin'
twenty mile to interrupt other people's range!   Well,
they 'camped right here, and *right here* THEY SEED
THE DEVIL!"

"Seed the Devil!" exclaimed Billy Teal.

"*Did* they, in right down airnest, now?" asked Jim
Waters, looking around at the dark woods, and insinuating himself between Abe Ludlow and the fire,
in evident fright.

"They seed the Devil," repeated Daddy Biggs,
with emphasis, "and ketcht him too!" he added;
"but they couldn't hold him."

"Good Gracious!" said Jim Waters, looking
around again—"do you think he stays about here?"
—and Jim got nearer to the fire.

"He stays about here *some*," replied Daddy Biggs.
"But Jim, son, get out from the fire!—you'll set
your over-halls afire!—and get me the sperrets.   I'll
buss the jug agin, and tell you all about it."

Bill Teal had deposited the jug behind a log, some
ten feet off; but Jim Waters was not the lad to back
out, if the Devil *was* about: so he made two despe-
rate strides and grabbed the "yeathen-war," and
then made two more, which brought him, head first,
jug and all, into the fire.   Chunks and sparks flew
everywhere, as he ploughed through!

"He's got you, Jim!" shouted Abe.

"Pull the boy out!" exclaimed Bill and myself in
a breath, "or he'll burn up!"

"Some on ye save the——*jug!*" screamed Daddy

Biggs, who was standing horror-stricken at the idea of being left without liquor in the woods.

In a minute both boy and jug were rescued; the former with burnt face and hands, and singed hair; the latter entirely uninjured.

"Well, well," chuckled Daddy Biggs, "we come outen *that* fust-rate—the jug aint hurt, nor no liquor spilt. But Jim, I'm raaly 'stonished at *you!* pitchin' in the fire that way, and you a-knowin' that was every drop o' sperrets we had!"

"Oh, but Daddy 'Lias," interposed Dick McCoy, "you must look over that—*he seed the Devil!*"

"Well, well, that 'minds me I was gwine to tell you all about that h—ll of a scrape I had wi' them Chatohospa fellows, last summer; so I'll squeeze the jug one time more, and tell you all about it."

Throwing his head into an admirable position for taking a view of things heavenly, Daddy Biggs inserted the mouth of the jug in his own mouth, when for a short space there was a sound which might be spelled, "*luggle–ugle–luggle–lul–uggle;*" and then Daddy Biggs set the jug down by him, and began his story once more.

"Well boys, they was 'camped right here, and had sot out their hooks for cat [fish], jist as we've done to night. Right thar, this side o' whar Bill's line hengs, some on 'em had tied a most a devil of a hook, from that big limb as goes strait out thar. He must a' had a kunnoo to fasten it whar he did, else cooned it on the top o' the limb. Well, it's allers swimmin' under that limb, but thar's a big rock, in the shape of a sugar-loaf, comes up in six inches o' the top. Right

Q

round *that* was whar I'd ketcht the monstousest, most oudaciousest Appeloosas cat, the week before, that ever come outen the Tallapoosy; and *they'd* hearn of it, and the fellow with the big hook was a fishin for hit's mate.   D—n it boys, it makes me mad to think how them Chatohospa fellows and the town folks do 'trude on we roover people, and when I'm aggra-wated I allers drinks, so here goes agin."

Daddy Biggs threw back his head again—again put the jug's mouth in his own—and again produced the sound of "guggle–uggle–lu–uggle!" and then resumed:

"This big-hook fellow I was tellin' about, his name were Jess Cole, which lives in the bottom, thar whar Chatohospa falls into the Hoota Locko; and aint got more'n half sense at that."

"'That's the fellow used to strike for Vince Kirk-land, in the blacksmith's shop at Dodd's, afore Vince died, aint it?" asked Bill Teal.

"That's him," said Daddy Biggs, "and that's how I come to know him, for I seed him thar once, tho' I can't say he know'd me.   Well, he waked up in the night, and heerd a most a h—ll of a sloshin' at the end of his line, and says he, 'Rise boys! I've got him! Durn my skin ef I hain't!'   And sure enough there was somethin' a flouncin' and sloshin', and makin' a devil of a conbobberation at the eend of the line. Jess he sprung up and got a long stick with a hook at one eend, and retched out and cotcht the line and tried to pull it in; but the thing on the hook give a flirt, and the stick bein' a leetle too short, which made him stoop forard, in *he* fell!   He scuffled out tho' tolloble quick, and ses he, 'boys, he's a whaler!—cuss my etarnal buttons if he aint the rise of sixty pounds! Old Biggs may go to h–ll *now* with his *forty-pound* cats, he can't shine no way!' When I heered that boys, I ——

"When *you* heerd it?" exclaimed all.

"Yes! *me!*" said Biggs laughingly; "didn't I tell you that before? Well, I oughter done it but forgot. D—n it, we'll take a drink on that, any way!" and so he did.

"So 'twas *you* instid o' the Devil, he cotched," observed Jim Waters, apparently much relieved by the disclosure.

"Jist so; and the way it was, I seed the rascals as they were comin' here, and knowed what they were arter. So when night comes, I slips down the roover bank mighty easy and nice, twell I could see the camp-fire. But thar was a dog along, and I was afraid to ventur up that way. See, I was after stealin' their fish they'd cotched thro' the day, which I knowd in reason they'd have a string on 'em in the water, at the kunnoo landin', to keep fresh. Well, seein' of the dog I 'cluded I'd 'tack the inimy by water, instid o' land. So with that I took the roover about thirty yards above here, and sure enough, finds the string of fish jist whar I knowed they'd be; and then I starts to swim down the roover a little ways, and git out below, and go to Jerry White's, and tell him the joke. Boys, aint you all gittin' mighty dry, *I* am."

And Daddy Biggs drank again!

"Well, boys, jist as I got whar that d—d hook was, not a thinkin' o' nuthin but the fun, the cussed

thang ketcht in one thigh of my over-hauls and brought
me up short.   I tried the cussedest ever a feller did
to get loose, *and* couldn't.   I had no knife, and thar
I flew round, and pulled first foraid and then backards, and reared and pitched, and made the water
bile.   Fact boys, I was " hitched to a swingin' limb,"
and no mistake.   Once or twice I got on the top of
the sugar-loaf rock, and *je-e-est* about the time I'd go
to untie the d—d rope of a line, the blasted rock was
so slippery *off I'd staunch!*—Fact boys!—And it aggrawated me; it aggrawated me *smartly,* so it did!
Ef I'd a' had liquor then, I'd a' took some, I was so
d—d mad! Well, in this time, that long-legged cuss,
Jess Cole, wakes up as I tell'd you, and hollers out
the way I norated.   Boys, what do you all say to another drink!   It makes me so *cussed* mad every time
I think 'bout it!"

Once more Daddy Biggs gazed at the stars!

" Yes, boys, it *does* make me mad.   But its *allers*
been so, ever sence I left old Pedee!   Fust I went
over to the Forky-Deer country—well! they driv me
off from *thar!*   Then I struck for the mountain country high up in Jurgy, and I finds me a place by the
side of a nice big krick; and thinks I, nobody never
kin pester me *here,* certain; for ef they git down in the
bottom, they'll be overflowed, and ef they ondertake
to bild housen on the hill-sides, they're so durned,
infernal steep, they'll have to *rope 'em to the trees!*
Well! what do you think?—hadn't been *thar* but
little better'n two year, afore they was as thick all
round me, as cuckle-burrs in a colt's tail, a-huntin
and a fishin all about me—and had bilt lanes—*lanes,*

i' God! every whar! So I flings the old 'oman 'cross a poney, and comes *here*—and I've bettered the thing mightily, to be sure, with this d—d scatter-gun crowd, from town and Chatohospa, a-makin the woods and roover farly roar from one day's eend to another—aint **I**? But, as I was a-sayin about that scrape I had wi' 'em—Soon as Jess said that about *his* cat bein' bigger'n *mine*, I said in my mind, ' I'll whip *you*, certin!' Well, they all kept a most a h–ll of a hollerin', and every now and then, some on 'em would throw a long log o' wood as they had cut for fire, as nigh at me as they could guess, *to stunt the cat*, you see; but the branches of the tree favoured me mightily in keepin' 'em off—tho' they'd hit pretty close by me 'casionally, ca-junk! strikin' eend-fore-most, you see. So *they* kept up a right smart throwin' o' logs, and *me*, a right peart dodgin', for some time; and I tell you, it took raal nice judgment to keep the infernal hook outen my meat; it grained the skin several times, as 'twas. At last, Jess he climbs into the tree and gits on the limb right over me, and ses he, ' boys, I b'lieve hit's a mud turkle, for I see some-thin' like the form o' one, right under me.' Thinks I, *you'll* find it one o' the *snappin'* sort, I judge. Then another one ses, ' thar's a way to try that, Jess, ef you see him;' and he hands Jess a gig. ' Now,' ses he, ' *gig him!* '"

" Gig THE DEVIL! ses I, for I *was* pestered!"

" Great G–d!" squalled Jess, "hit's the Devil!" and down *he* tumbled right a top o' me! I thought I was busted open from one eend to 'tother! Sure enough tho', I warn't, but only busted loose from the

line.   Both on us put for the bank quick, but on account of my gittin' holt of the gig, which ruther
bothered me, Jess got ashore fust.   I was *right arter
him* tho', I tell you, *with the gig!*   When I clum up
the bank, I found the rest was all kleen gone, and
thar lay Jess, which had stumped his toe agin' somethin', right flat of his face, a-moanin' dreadful!

"Oh, I've got you *now*, Jess," ses I.

"Please Devil!" ses Jess.

"Must take you along wi' me," ses I, in the
d—dest most onyeathly voice you *ever* heered.

"The hogs I took warn't *marked*," ses Jess, a-shi-
verin' all over.

"They warn't *yourn*," ses I.

"I'll never do so no more," ses Jess, shiverin'
wuss and wuss, "ef you'll let me off this time."

"Can't do it, Jess; want you down in Tophet, *to
strike for Vince Kirkland*.   I've got *him* thar, a-
blacksmithin' of it.   He does all my odd jobs, like
pinetin' of my tail and sich like!   Can't let you off—
I've come a purpose for you!"

"I seed the poor devil shudder when I called
Vince's name, but he didn't say no more, so I jobs
the gig thro' the hind part of his overhauls and starts
down to the kunnoo landin' with him, in a peart trot.
The way he scratched up the dirt as he travelled
backards on his all-fours, was a perfect sight!   But
jist as I struck the roover, he got holt of a grub, and
the gig tore out, *and he started 'tother way!*   I never
seed runnin' twell *then*—'taint no use to try to tell
you how fast he *did* run; I couldn't do it in a week.
A "scared wolf," warn't nothin' to him.   He run

And their las loss, which had stumped his toe agin somethin right flat
I his face a-mcanin' dreadfl

faster'n six scared wolves and a yearlin' deer. Soon
as he got a start I made for a log whar I seed their
guns, and behind that I finds the big powder gourd
they all kept their powder in that they warn't a-usin'.
Thinks I, ef you aint all *kleen* gone, I'll finish the job
for you; so I pitched the gourd—it hilt fully a gallon
—smack into the fire, and then jumped in the roover
myself. I hadn't more'n got properly in before it
blowed up. Sich a blaze I never seed before. The
n'ise was some itself, but the blaze covered all creation, and retched higher than the trees. It spread
out to the logs whar the guns was, and fired *them* off!
Pop! pop! pop! No wonder them Chatohospa fellows never come back! Satan, hisself, couldn't a
done it no better, ef he had been thar, in the way of
racket and n'ise!"

Daddy Biggs now took a long breath, and a longer
drink.

"Boys," he then added, "I got them fellers' fish
and a two-gallon jug o' sperrets, and I throwed their
guns in the roover, besides givin' 'em the all-gortiest
scare they ever had; and they aint been back sence,
which I hope they never will, for its oudacious the
way the roover folks is 'posed upon. And now,
boys, that's my ' scrape;' so less take another drink,
look at the hooks, and then lay down!"

Stereotyped by J. C. D. Christman & Co.,
Philadelphia.